THE MANAGEMENT
OF WORKING CAPITAL

THE MANAGEMENT
OF WORKING CAPITAL

James McN. Stancill, Jr.
Graduate School of Business
University of Southern California

61313

Intext Educational Publishers
Scranton   *Toronto*   *London*

International's Series in

FINANCIAL MANAGEMENT

ISBN   0-7002-2370-3

Copyright © 1971 by International Textbook Company

Library of Congress Catalog Card No. 73-132908

To Catherine,

Martha, Mary, and Christine

Editor's Note

The International Textbook Series in Financial Management was designed with three purposes in mind. First, to provide textbooks for university-level courses with primary emphasis on financial decision making. Second, to provide the financial practitioner with technical information and decision-making techniques. Third, to permit maximum flexibility in course and curriculum design within the broader scope of financial management. In this regard a large selection of original works will be offered, high in intellectual quality and content. All materials offered in the series will deal with the broadening scope of the field of financial management, the theoretical foundations, the relevant intra- and interdisciplinary nature of the facets of the financial management field, the influence of modern analytical decision-oriented techniques, and the decision-making aspects of financial management problems.

The general pace of the evolution of thought in the field of financial management has recently accelerated. Significant innovations have added new complexity to the field of financial management and existing problems are being met with new approaches. Moreover, as the technology advances, the traditional lines of demarcation become indistinguishable between such areas as institutional finance, financial management, investments, and money and capital markets. Since these intra-disciplinary interactions affect the analysis of complex problems, they are now attracting attention from both scholars and practitioners. Hence the need for a series with appeal for both groups. Moreover, tools of analysis from economics, mathematics, statistics, computer science, and behavioral science are being applied to these problems. Topics covered in each volume place primary emphasis on these tools of analysis in an intra-disciplinary setting.

Contents

CHAPTER 1

Introduction

As with modern computers, the field of business finance may also be said to be entering its "third generation." At first, business finance consisted primarily of description and analysis of financing instruments. Following World War II, the emphasis shifted to the "managerial" approach. Through the use of text and cases, the reader was asked to project himself into the position of a finance manager and, learning from others, to make decisions that seemed appropriate. While an improvement on the former approach, this phase still lacked the rigor that was characteristic of other fields of economics, and—equally important—seemed oblivious to the usefulness of quantitative techniques, even the simplest ones.

With the rise of operations research as an aid in business decision making, it was only natural that more rigorous and analytical tools should be brought to bear on what now has become the *economics of finance.* While articles in professional journals devoted to finance were leading the way, it remained for men like Professors William Beranek and Myron Gordon to usher in the new era—Beranek with his *Analysis for Financial Decisions* (1963),[1] and Gordon, a year earlier, with his work *The Investment, Financing and Valuation of the Corporation.*[2]

While utilizing the same analytical approach as Beranek, Gordon's work did not treat the full array of business finance topics as did Beranek. In 1966 two new textbooks appeared which attempted to integrate the new "economics of finance" and place it at the disposal of students of finance.[3]

---

[1]William Beranek, *Analysis for Financial Decisions* (Homewood, Ill.: Irwin, 1963). Henceforth this work will be referred to as Beranek's *Analysis.*
[2]Myron J. Gordon, *The Investment, Financing and Valuation of the Corporation* (Homewood, Ill.: Irwin, 1962).
[3]See S. H. Archer and C. A. D'Ambrosio, *Business Finance: Theory and Management* (New York: Macmillan, 1966), and Seymour Friedland, *The Economics of Corporate Finance* (Englewood Cliffs, N. J.: Prentice-Hall, 1966).

Also deserving of recognition were two books that were decidedly ahead of their times: J. B. Williams, *The Theory of Investment Value* (Cambridge: Harvard University Press, 1938), and B. B. Howard and Miller Upton, *Introduction to Business Finance* (New York: McGraw-Hill, 1953). Lerner and Carleton's monograph, *A Theory of Financial Analysis* (New York: Harcourt, Brace & World, 1966) has also contributed significantly to advancing the theory of finance, particularly in a mathematical context.[4],[5].

It is my intention, therefore, to continue working this same vein, and in some way to clarify former techniques or to develop new approaches to that part of the economics of finance that we call *working capital management.*

THE MEANING OF THE MANAGEMENT OF WORKING CAPITAL

The topics covered in the economics of finance may generally be classified as follows: (a) asset management, (b) financial forecasting and control, (c) financing the firm, and (d) the so-called "special topics," such as dividend policy, reorganization, or valuation and merger. While omitting the special-topics category, this book will treat the first three with the following exceptions: (i) The management of long-term or "fixed" assets. While rightly a part of "asset management," this topic has taken on a literature of its own and is called "capital budgeting." (ii) Intermediate and long-term financing, a thorough treatment of which would easily cover a volume itself. (iii) Financial forecasting will be limited in discussion—but not implication—to cash flows deriving from the regular operation of the firm.

Thus "management of working capital" will be construed to mean the management of cash, marketable securities, accounts receivable, and inventory, and the financing of these assets. In short, this will be a study of *current assets* and *current liabilities,* and their associated cash flows.

The term "management of current assets" is used to describe the process by which optimization of these assets is realized—or at least

[4]Undoubtedly I am remiss for not including other significant books in this brief recital of efforts that have contributed to the third-generation approach. I only hope the reader will acknowledge these omissions as oversights and not an attempt to deliberately skip over certain works.

[5]Lerner and Carleton's book also has a succinct section on "incorporating economics into financial analysis." (Ibid., pp. 4–11.)

attempts at determining optimum levels will be made. For many firms the old-fashioned flying by the seat of the pants is no longer good enough. Instead, the finance manager is being pressed to keep assets at levels consistent with the firm's goals, or—stated alternatively—to maintain optimum levels of assets for a given profit objective.

The determination of the *optimum level* for these various asset accounts varies, however. The desired volume of cash and marketable securities will be approached directly while the volume of accounts receivable and inventory will be derived indirectly as a result of the exercise of numerous decision rules on the various components of the asset accounts.

PLAN OF THE BOOK

While largely theoretical, the specific treatment applied to each topic will be, generally, the identification of the relevant variables in the problem and the construction of a model with the derivation of decision rules based on the model. Because of space limitations we do not include a thorough explanation of the design and meaning of all aspects of model building, but a brief summary of the more relevant aspects follows.[6]

Goals of the Firm

Throughout this book the assumption will be made that the firm is seeking to maximize profit in the long run, *and*—quite importantly—to survive. Whenever this type of statement is made, questions are at once invited as to what is meant by *maximize* and *in the long run.* Perhaps the best reply is to say what I do *not* mean, viz., maximizing does not mean "at all costs." The rule of reason must prevail, and any poliferation of what *maximize* means would be an interesting intellectual effort, but solely out of place here. *In the long run* implies the antithesis of a "milking" objective—"get what we can, and run."

While the maximum-profit assumption is made in this book, it would be naive to assume that this is the only goal motivating American businessmen. Other possible goals might be the "reasonable profit" goal.

[6]An excellent discussion of business goals, decision, and models is contained in Chapters 1 and 2 of Beranek's *Analysis.* Cf. also Russell L. Ackoff, *The Design of Social Research* (Chicago: Un. of Chicago Press, 1953), especially Chapters I, II, III, and V; K. J. Cohen and R. M. Cyert, *The Theory of the Firm* (New York, Prentice-Hall, 1965), Parts I and III; and H. Bierman, L. Fouraker, and R. Jaedicke, *Quantitative Analysis for Business Decisions* (Homewood, Ill.: Irwin, 1965), Chapters 1 and 3 and *passim.*

This usually means that the owner is making "enough," and doesn't really wish to push for additional profits. Market position is another commonly found goal. Or, there is the case of the "largest in the . . ." goal. In this case the entrepreneur consciously sets out to become the largest automobile dealer, the largest orange grower, or whatever, in his area, in the state, in the nation. In these cases, incidentally, it is reasonable to assume that being the largest does not mean necessarily being the most profitable. But for some individuals the ego-pleasing phrase "I am the largest" is much more important than the additional profits that he might realize at, possibly, a lower level of sales.[7]

Large listed corporations are almost always profit-oriented, but for many "maximum profits" would be overstating their goals. For many, maintaining the stock price and/or the dividend coverage takes on tremendous importance.

For practical purposes, this book does not try explicitly to ascertain the exact goal of a firm; instead, if the firm is desirous of making more profit by better utilization of its working capital then its goal may be said to be consistent with the assumptions of each chapter.

Decisions and Decision Criteria

On the assumption that the firm does have a goal, it is reasonable to assume further that decisions within the firm—and particularly financial decisions—will be made consistent with the announced (or assumed) goal or goals. But decisions need not be consistent with the primary goal, and in fact many are not. An optimum decision will be understood to infer consistency with the primary goal.

Suboptional decisions are decisions made at levels lower than presidential or top management levels, and, presumably, are effected to achieve a course of action consistent with the primary goals. In either case, however, it is important to assess the *decision criteria* to ascertain whether or not they are consistent with the primary goal of the firm.

Certainty, Risk, and Uncertainty

Whenever a decision is made, it may be said to be made under conditions of certainty, risk, or uncertainty. Certainty implies that there is one—and only one—outcome to the course of action selected. In the

---

[7]The economic theory of the firm has a great deal of difficulty in handling goals of a "nonprofit maximizing nature." On this point, however, see Sidney Weintraub, *Price Theory* (New York: Pitman, 1949), pp. 151–154.

real business world, conditions of certainty are practically never found. Almost invariably there are two or more possible outcomes to any decision. But in the process of analysis, it is sometimes useful to *assume* at first that the decision will be made in a condition of certainty. But once the elements of the decision are identified, it is usually necessary to interject the other possible outcomes into the decision.

When the other outcomes are known, and it is possible to compute or guess at the probability of occurrence of such outcomes, the decision is being made under the condition of *risk*. If it is possible to compute the probability of occurrence, this type of probability is known as *objective* or *frequence* probability. For example, if sufficient data exist to show that one out of fifty accounts of a certain description never pay their bills, then we are dealing with objective probability. But there are other cases when the decision maker, using his personal knowledge and background, must guess at the probability of occurrence. In these cases he would be dealing with *subjective* or *Bayesian* probabilities. If it is not possible to define the limits of all outcomes or the probability of occurrence then the decision maker is dealing with a state of *uncertainty*. In such cases, since a decision must be made, it may be necessary to make some assumption for example *all* outcomes are equally likely. At other times it may be practical to simulate possible outcomes and thus derive an insight into the possible outcomes.[8]

Variables and Parameters

Loosely defined, *variables* are the identifiable elements of a problem; the "things" that are to be manipulated in order to effect a decision. *Parameters*, on the other hand, are constraints within which the problem (or solution) will take place. Generally speaking, parameters in a business situation must be accepted as so much exogenous data. It is possible, however, for something to be a variable in one situation, and a parameter in another, for example, the state of the economy.

---

[8]All of the above remarks, of course, assume that it is worthwhile to make an optimal decision. If it does not make any difference how a decision is made, the problem is obviated. Furthermore, the dollar volume involved may not justify the effort to arrive at a rational decision. On the matter of probabilistic decision making, there are many competent sources that might be cited, but Bierman *et al.*, *op. cit.*, Chapters 2 and 4 contain an excellent review. Sometimes it becomes a matter of importance to ascertain "how much" a firm is willing to pay to gain (additional) information on which to base a decision. On this, see chapter 22, *ibid.*, and B. O. Koopman and G. E. Kimball, "Information Theory," in *Notes on Operations Research* (Cambridge: Technology Press, 1959).

Mean Estimates and Variance

In the handling and manipulation of variables it is important to be cognizant of the derivation of such estimates. *Point estimates*, vis-à-vis *range estimates*, are sometimes derived from the *mean* (average) of a distribution. If the term "expected" mean is used it connotes the probabilistic weighting of the observations (or items) of the distribution. Thus

$$\overline{X}_E = \sum_{i=1}^{n} \frac{X(P_x)}{n} \tag{1-1}$$

is not the same as a simple mean, $\overline{X}$. Weighting, often by Bayesian probabilities, has been found to be a significant improvement over unweighted averages and can be used in a number of business problems.

While point estimates will represent the average, or weighted average, it is often useful to secure estimates of the dispersion about the average. For this, the variance or some variation of the variance will be used. Mathematically, the sample variance, s^2, is

$$s^2 = \sum_{i}^{n} \frac{(X - \overline{X})^2}{n} \tag{1-2}$$

Usually, however, the square root of the variance is used as a measure of dispersion, and this is called the *standard deviation*. Thus

$$s = \sqrt{\sum_{i}^{n} \frac{(X - \overline{X})^2}{n}} \tag{1-3}$$

Sometimes it is necessary to secure an "unbiased" estimate of the variance or standard deviation in which case the expression $n - 1$ is used instead of n. Note also that Phoenician (here italic) letters are used for *sample* statistics (a subset of the whole) while Greek letters are used for statistics of the whole population. Thus μ and σ would be the mean and standard deviation for the population (whole set), or sometimes for a parameter.

If the dispersion of a distribution *relative* to a mean is desired, the *coefficient of variation* (CV) is used. Thus

$$CV = \frac{s}{\overline{X}} \tag{1-4}$$

Frequently, the CV is used as a measure of *risk*, i.e., if there was a *certain* outcome, $s = 0$ and thus $CV = 0$. The greater the dispersion about a mean, i.e., the more the risk, then the higher the CV (expressed as a percentage).

If *range estimates* (RE), or *confidence limits* of a distribution are sought, standard practice indicates that the range be specified as so many (usually three) standard deviations from the mean. Thus

$$RE_x = \overline{X} \pm y(s) \tag{1-5}$$

where $y =$ the number of standard deviations desired. If there is a "normal" distribution, ± 3 standard deviations will include about 99 percent of the cases.

If a *subjective* estimate of s is desired, then merely dividing the (subjective) range by *six* will produce a crude estimate of s. Sometimes even subjective estimates of s, say, for use in a CV, are better than merely verbalizing on the relative dispersion.

Models

Models are the structure into which variables are put. Variables are the "ingredients" of the model. But since there has arisen a degree of mysticism concerning the word *model*, it may be well to be more specific in the definition of the term. A model is a formal relationship—almost any structured formal relationship may be called a model. It may be an equation, a graphic depiction, or even the format of a set of data—for example, a cash-flow model.

Decision Rules and Strategies

While a model is a logical structure of variables, the *purpose* of the model is usually to derive a *decision rule*, i.e., a guide to a course of action that will be optimal, minimal, or maximum as the case may be. In cases where a model is used to select one of several courses of action, it is usually called a strategy, but *decision rule* and *strategy* are used interchangeably so frequently that the reader is cautioned against making sharp semantical differences between the two.

CHAPTER **2**

Cash Management*

Of all the asset accounts of a firm, the cash and marketable securities accounts are usually the only ones solely under the discretion of the finance manager. After reviewing the present and past treatments of the management of cash and marketable securities, a model is presented which attempts to provide a workable answer to the elusive question of how much a firm should carry in cash and marketable securities.

THE TRADITIONAL APPROACH TO CASH MANAGEMENT

The earliest approaches to cash management[1] were couched in terms of ratio analysis and were epitomized by the adage that a firm should keep so many days' worth of payables in their cash account or a certain percentage of sales. Thirty days or two weeks come to mind as rather typical rules of thumb.[2] If a percentage of sales approach was taken, then the industry average was usually suggested. In other cases the discussion of "How much?" was answered only in the most general way by stating some of the most basic determinants of the cash balance (such as "It depends on the industry") or stating that cash should be sufficient to pay the bills as they accrue.[3] But this ratio approach suffers from the same

---

*This chapter is based largely on my article, "The Determination of Corporate Holdings of Cash and Marketable Securities," in Edward J. Mock (ed.) *Financial Decision Making* (Scranton, Pa.: International Textbook Company, 1967), pp. 269–283.

[1] In this chapter the word "cash" is meant to define the firm's demand deposit (checking) account at a bank. Currency on hand will be referred to as "till cash," and marketable securities will include those securities which a firm holds as "near-cash" items. Later each of these categories will be accorded separate treatment. The composition of the marketable securities portfolio is treated in Chapter 3.

[2] At least twenty basic finance and accounting texts published in the 1920's and early 1930's were checked for an explicit citation, but either the subject of cash was ignored or only a passing perfunctory reference was made to it.

8

deficiencies as all ratio analyses. "What is" is construed to be "What should be."

Following this "descriptive" or ratio approach, some basic textbooks in corporation finance adopted a Keynesian "liquidity preference" approach.[4] In the framework of Keynes' General Theory,[5] the motives for holding cash were trichotomized as (1) transactions balances, (2) speculative balances, and (3) precautionary balances. A fourth motive, the "finance" motive, was added by Keynes in a later article.[6] Expressed in corporate finance terms, these motives may be roughly defined, in order, as (1) the cash balances needed to transact the day-to-day activities of the firm, (2) balances set aside in anticipation of price declines (of inventory items, for example), (3) "safety stocks"—balances motivated by possible business declines, and (4) those cash balances set aside in anticipation of a major expenditure—for example, an extraordinary capital budgeting item.

While of questionable value in explaining the theory of interest,[7] this approach helps, in a theoretical way, to explain why firms hold cash, but it is quite insufficient in establishing *how much* cash to hold.

As shown in Figure 2-1, the usual depiction of the liquidity-preference function, the cash balance is shown to be an inverse function of the interest rate, *i*. But is it? As Hicks pointed out in an article in 1937,[8] the "transactions" demand for cash, L_1, presumes a given interest rate. Thus Keynes was guilty of the logical error of *hysteron proteron*, or more simply, circularity. From a more pragmatic approach, however, Keynes' theory, while introspectively plausible, seems to ignore businessmen's

---

[3]Dauten, for example, made the following statement in his finance text: "In determining the amount of cash which a business needs, it is necessary to understand fully all of the factors that affect the cash account and to consider the effect which the trend, the seasonal, and the irregular movements have on each of them." Carl A. Dauten, *Business Finance* (Englewood Cliffs, N. J.: Prenctice-Hall, 1948), p. 292.

[4]Cf. Pearson Hunt et al., *Basic Business Finance*, rev. ed. (Homewood, Ill.: Irwin, 1961), pp. 89–90, and more recently Seymour Friedland, *The Economics of Corporate Finance* (Englewood Cliffs, N.J.: Prentice-Hall, 1966), pp. 99–119. Others, e.g., Alvin F. Donaldson and J. K. Pfahl, *Corporate Finance* (New York, Ronald, 1963), p. 482, and J. Fred Weston, *Managerial Finance* (New York: Holt, 1962), pp. 98–99, while not following the Keynesian terminology, couch their explanation of the desirable cash balance in motivational terms (i.e., the motives for holding cash such as for "safety stocks" or "financing stocks."

[5]John M. Keynes, *The General Theory of Employment, Interest and Money.* (New York: Harcourt, 1935), p. 170.

[6]John M. Keynes, "Alternative Theories of the Rate of Interest," *Economic Journal*, January 1937, pp. 241–252.

[7]At least in today's world of an institutionalized capital market.

[8]J. R. Hicks, "Mr. Keynes and the 'Classics': a Suggested Interpretation," *Econmetrical*, April 1937, pp. 147–159.

thinking with respect to their cash and marketable securities account. Admittedly, at *very* low short-term rates of interest, businessmen may be reluctant or slow to switch redundant cash into marketable securities, and at high rates they may be more conscious of the opportunity cost of retaining redundant cash. But to give short-term interest rates a place of dominant importance in a theory that attempted to be *positive* in nature is unrealistic. Keynes' liquidity-preference theory simply ignores the indigenous factors at work within the firm.

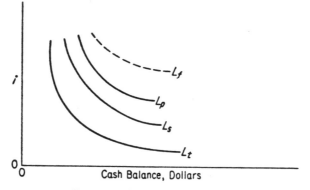

Figure 2-1. Liquidity preference.

Tackling just the transactions demand for cash by business firms, Baumol, Beranek, and more recently Whalen have developed some interesting models to attempt to answer the "how much" aspect of the subject. Baumol[9] attempted a union between "inventory theory and monetary theory"[10] in a mathematical model—but without explicit recognition of probabilistic variance. In general, Baumol concludes that even in a stationary state "some" cash should be held and, secondly, "that the transactions demand for cash will vary approximately in proportion with the money value of transactions."[11]

Beranek[12] like Baumol, dealt only with the "transactions demand" for cash, but advanced his model in a probabilistic framework. In particular, Beranek's work is commendable for this probabilistic approach and

[9]William J. Baumol, "The Transactions Demand for Cash: An Inventory Theoretic Approach," *Quarterly Journal of Economics,* November 1952, pp. 545–556.

[10]*Ibid.,* p. 545.

[11]In other words, if cash balances were used as a regressor with sales, the slope of the regression line would be positive and approximately unitary.

[12]William Beranek, *Analysis, op. cit.,* pp. 345–387.

for isolating salient variables in the process of determining a firm's cash balance. In his words, the "Factors in the decision are (1) behavior and magnitude of cash flows, (2) size of 'critical' minimum, (3) amount of 'short' cost, (4) returns from marketable securities, and (5) length of cash balance planning period."[13] The "short cost" comes about when the balance falls below the "critical minimum" and is defined to consist of the cash discount foregone on the firm's accounts payable, and the deterioration in credit rating.[14] To include these two aspects of the "short cost" in his probabilisitc model of the "critical balance," Beranek had to quantify each, and in so doing made his model difficult to apply. It is unrealistic to suggest that a firm quantify "deteriorioation in credit" position. Credit position is a function of many variables, and to isolate this variable in a "transactions balances only" approach is theoretically convenient but a gross simplification. Also unrealistic is the presumption that cash discounts will be forgone if the critical balance is violated. This may indeed happen, but for a well-managed firm short-term loans are a less costly alternative.

Edmund Whalen, the third author cited, tried to follow up Baumol's work and directed his paper[15] to an empirical examination of whether the mechanistic assumption of the more pure Keynesian liquidity-preference theory (the relationship between the transactions and the precautionary balances) or the Baumol[16]-Tobin[17] approach, which set forth nonproportionate hypotheses,[18] was more plausible. In short, "Do transactions and precautionary cash balances of nonfinancial business corporations vary proportionately or less than in proportion to changes in the volume of their sales?"[19]

In this macro approach, Whelan's findings seem to indicate that cash balances in some industries appear to increase "more than in proportion to sales." While of interest, this study still leaves the determination of a realistic, micro approach to the determination of a firm's cash and marketable securities balance unanswered. It is only normative, i.e., it deals

[13] *Ibid.*, p. 385.
[14] *Ibid.*, pp. 385, 360–362.
[15] Edward L. Whalen, "A Cross-Section Study of Business Demand for Cash," *Journal of Finance*, September 1965, pp. 423–443.
[16] Baumol, *loc. cit.*
[17] James Tobin, "The Interest Elasticity of Transactions Demand for Cash," *Review of Economics and Statistics*, August 1956, pp. 241–247.
[18] Or, in the jargon of economic theory, "nonunitary elasticity."
[19] Whalen, *loc. cit.*, p. 423.

with "what is" rather than "what should be." It is a worthwhile study, however, and should provide ground for further empirical examinations at a macroeconomic level.

Delineating the Problem

All firms are faced with the problem of how much to keep as till cash and how much to keep in their checking account at a bank—although too many firms are unwilling to rigorously face up to the problem. For those firms that pass a certain point in their development where they are considered "middle-sized" or "large," a third aspect must be reckoned with—investment in marketable securities.[20] For some firms, a separate payroll and/or dividend account is maintained, and since this is a logical subset of the whole problem an approach to the management of this account will be suggested.

For most nonfinancial, noncommercial firms, the problem of how much to keep in "till cash," i.e., their cash registers or cash drawers, is of substantially less magnitude than the other two aspects of the problem. While till cash will be ignored for the rest of this book, it is hoped that more rigorous, stochastic reasoning will be devoted to the matter where relevant.

With respect to the demand deposit (general corporate checking) account—and what will henceforth be called the *cash* account—the usual purposes for maintaining it are: (1) to use it to pay "accounts payable," and (2) to use it for a depository for the checks received through the firm's credit sales—"accounts receivable." When payroll checks are issued, often a charge is made to the general account and the amount of the payroll deposited in a separate payroll account—usually at the same bank (or banks) as the general account. Lacking perfect synchronization in the inflows and outflows of the general account, all firms find that the desira-

---

[20]This is so because most money-market instruments come "packaged" in rather large denominations, e.g., $10,000, $50,000, or even $100,000. To buy such instruments a firm needs, perforce, rather substantial sums. I hasten to add, however, that "marketable securities" should be construed to include all *interest-bearing* or *dividend-paying* assets— Treasury bills, commercial paper, certificates of deposit (CD's), deposits in savings and loans, time deposits, and certain stocks. In this respect, therefore, even small firms may have marketable securites in the form of deposits in their local savings bank or a time (savings) deposit at their bank. Furthermore, the model suggested and the discussion in this chapter could include the problem faced by small firms, too. Chapter 3 deals extensively with money-market instruments.

ble balance is other than zero—the theoretically most profitable balance because no money is earned on demand deposits.

The purpose of maintaining a marketable-securities account is assumed in this book to be an interest-earning cushion which could be used to sop up redundant cash or, alternately, to supplement cash when the account dips below the optimal level. With this purpose in mind, consideration will not be given to a determination of how much "other" securities (subsequently defined as "free" marketable securities) a firm may happen to have included in its balance-sheet item "marketable securities."[21] Payroll, tax payments, and extraordinary purchases (e.g., a building, a major capital expenditure, or a purchase of another firm) are factors to reckon with, and subsequently will be included in the discussion of the question.

Stated as directly as possible, a firm must have *enough* in its cash account to meet the claims presented against such account. This does not mean that for every dollar in checks written (or drawn) today there must be a dollar on deposit. Not at all! Barring a state law to the contrary, a firm must have *on deposit* only the amount *presented* (charged) to its account. This is true also of the firm's payroll account, and failure to be aware of this might result in the maintenance of an excessive amount in the cash (or payroll) account. Similarly, the amount held in the marketable securities account should be enough to absorb the usual shocks in the cash account, but the rest ("free" marketable securities) should be put to use more profitably to finance other accounts, e.g., inventories, receivables, or fixed assets. If opportunities for investment in these other assets —and for most viable firms this implies at greater rates of return than are usually realizable in marketable securities—are not available at any point in time, then the marketable-securities account would swell to that extent. But what is the "unneeded" (free) amount in this account? Furthermore, how should the optimal amount be determined? Likewise, what is the optimal cash balance for a firm at any point in time, and how should this amount be determined? To seek a deterministic approach to these questions it is first necessary to deal with the optimal cash balance for it is the cash account (or rather the behavior of the cash account) that logically should determine the marketable securities balance.

---

[21]It is because of this "grossing" problem, i.e., the inclusion of marketable securities —for the above-mentioned purpose—and "other," e.g., investment securities, in the balance-sheet account that empirical studies utilizing published statements only are on questionable ground.

DETERMINING THE OPTIMAL CASH BALANCE

In order to approach the question of how much to have in a cash account, it is useful to categorize the various inflows and outflows in the account. While not pretending to be exhaustive, the following seem to be the most common and important:[22]

1. Inflows
   A. Accounts Receivable
   B. "Cash sales" receipts

2. Outflows
   A. Accounts payable
   B. Taxes
   C. Payroll
   D. Extraordinary expenditures,
      e.g., large capital outlays

Further classifications of these accounts, however, suggests this dichotomization:

Random variables
   1A. Accounts receivable
   1B. Cash sales
   2A. Accounts payable

Controllable (known)
variables
   2B. Taxes
   2C. Payroll
   2D. Extraordinary expenditures
   2E. Cash dividends

Viewing the activity of the cash account in this way, the problem resolves to this: (i) have enough cash to compensate for the *lack of perfect synchronization* in the random variables (the inflows and the outflows), and (ii) provide a way in which 2B, 2C, 2D, and 2E expenditures (controllable outflows) can be "covered," i.e., a balance sufficient to take care of

---

[22]A somewhat similar approach was taken by Archer and D'Ambrosio (Stephen H. Archer and Charles D'Ambrosio, *Business Finance: Theory and Management,* New York: Macmillan, 1966, p. 331) in their treatment of the management of cash. I am particularly indebted to Professor Archer for stimulating my interest in this subject and for providing a useful framework of analysis, particularly with respect to the payroll model presented later in this chapter.

the random, routine activity *and* these substantial but controllable (known?) withdrawals.

Assuming daily rectification of the cash account at the bank, and that the bank posts deposits before withdrawals, if the inflows were exactly equal to the outflows the account could be opened with $1, and this would be the daily closing balance. Since this is not the case, obviously, what the firm really must do is to provide for the *dissynchronization* of these inflows and outflows. To do this, it is possible to construct a probability distribution of the firm's day-to-day *change* in their cash account *sans* the amounts attributable to the "controllable variable" items. Of course this distribution should be as independent as possible of seasonal factors, such as Christmas, Easter, and the Fall "busy" period. To do this it appears possible to take separate periods (by seasons, for example) and construct a distribution for each season, or to devise a "seasonal index" that could be used as a deflator or inflator for each season's activity. Figure 2-2 illustrates the former approach.

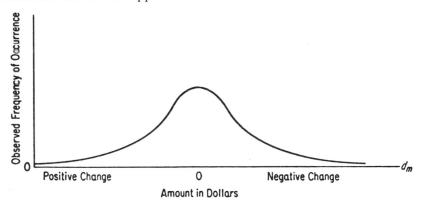

Figure 2-2. Day-to-day change in cash account after removal of "controllable" changes in the account. [This distribution would not be a continuous function, but rather a discrete one. It is shown as continuous for purposes of exposition and convenience only.]

Having constructed such a distribution, our next problem is to formulate a decision rule for the daily opening balance. Since the major problem is not having sufficient cash, we are concerned with the negative side only. If the opening balance is greater than the desired opening balance, the excess[23] may be used to purchase marketable securities.

[23]More specifically, the excess beyond a second amount somewhat greater than the desired opening balance. This is the "indifference band" and is discussed in the next section.

Looking therefore at the "negative change" side of the distribution, a first approximation to the optimal cash balance, which is now called the desired opening balance, may be had by deciding on the *chance* to be taken of not having enough cash on any given day (Figure 2-3). If, for example, management elects to take a 1 percent chance of "running short," its *decision rule* is found by merely selecting that dollar amount to the right of which includes 1 percent of the observations.

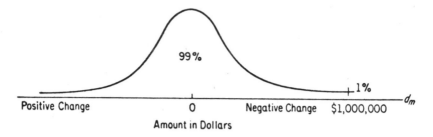

Figure 2-3. Illustration of the decision rule for the desired opening balance.

The *larger* the desired opening balance, the *smaller* the chance of running short, and vice versa. Exactly what dollar limit the firm selects as its decision rule would be a function of many factors, but the two that seem of greatest moment are (i) management's aversion to a tight cash situation, and (ii), on a more *ad hominem* basis, the relationship the firm has with the bank. If, for example, the bank is made cognizant of what the firm is trying to do, it might agree to give the firm until the next morning to sell some marketable securities and through, say, telegraphic transfer or even intrabank transfer thus cover the deficiency.[24]

If it is possible to establish a line of credit with a bank that would automatically become effective with an overdraft, the absolute size of the desired opening balance could be lowered. This implies, of course, a greater chance of running short of cash. This backup line of credit would be most advisable if the firm did not have marketable securities in a sufficient amount as described below. One very progressive bank, with which the author is familiar, has developed a model of this type for its customers' convenience.

[24]With the current state of competition among banks this is not an unrealistic suggestion. Furthermore, the oft-expressed suggestion after World War II that firms should keep healthy balances with their bank is now quite unrealistic.

If perchance the firm has a loan agreement with the bank to maintain a minimum-level balance, this situation could be accounted for by *raising* the desired opening balance to meet this restriction. If this balance is less than the desired opening balance, the desired opening balance amount should supersede the smaller "required" amount.

The Indifference Band

Primarily because of the cost of effecting a purchase of marketable securities (say Treasury bills), the desired opening balance should be construed to be the lower limit of a range—called the *indifference band*. The width of the band is thus a function of this transaction (purchase) cost, translated into the daily interest on a given increment of marketable securities. On a $100,000 lot of Treasury bills, the daily interest is, currently, approximately $16–$20. If the cost of making a purchase is construed to be $15, then the width of the indifference band would thus be about $100,000.

Viewing the lower limit of this indifference band as the "reorder point," we see that the problem of the width of the band has some aspects of an inventory problem. In fact, Miller and Orr[25] have considered this to be the case and applied an EOQ (economic order quantity)—square root—formula for the solution. To do this, however, they have to assume a "purchase cost," as was done above, and, additionally, a constant issuance rate. The cost of carrying the inventory is, or course, the daily interest lost—$16 to $20 on a $100,000 block of bills in the above example. The trouble with this approach, however, is that it is unreasonable to assume a constant issuance—i.e., withdrawal or decrease in the cash account. Miller and Orr go well beyond this naive approach, however, and have developed an interesting stochastic model for the width of the band and the desired cash balance.

Cash is allowed to vary in the cash account until it hits an upper limit h, at which time securities are bought (in an amount of hz) in order to reduce the balance to z, which represents what Miller and Orr call the *return point* and is similar to d_m. If the balance falls below z, no action is taken until a dollar balance r is reached. At that point, money-market securities are sold in an amount rz in order to return the balance to the level z.

In the Miller and Orr model,

$$z = \left(\frac{3\gamma \sigma^2}{4v} \right)^{\frac{1}{3}} \tag{2-1}$$

$$h = 3z \tag{2-2}$$

[25] Merton H. Miller and Daniel Orr, "A Model of the Demand for Money by Firms," *Quarterly Journal of Economics*, August 1966, pp. 413–435.

for the special case where p = the probability that the cash balance will increase = .5, and q = the probability that the cash balance will decrease =.5. In the above equation σ^2 represents the variance of the daily change in the cash balance, γ = cost per transfer (presumably either into cash or into securities), and v = daily interest rate on securities.[26]

The object of the Miller and Orr model is to minimize the cost function ϵ (c) by choice of the variables z and h. The cost function[27] is defined as

$$\epsilon(c) = \gamma \frac{\epsilon(N)}{T} + v \ \epsilon \ (M) \tag{2-3}$$

where $\epsilon(N)$ = expected number of transfers between cash account and marketable securities during the upcoming period

T = number of days in period

$\epsilon(M)$ = expected average daily balance

Provision for Controllable Variables

The term "first approximation" of the desired opening balance was used above advisedly, however, for the preceding model accounts only for what was described as random-variable flows. How could the firm provide for the controllable-variable amounts, such as taxes, payroll, dividends, and capital expenditures? If the firm wants strictly to observe the profit motive it should provide for such demands, which presumably would be through a gradual accumulation, by increases earmarked for such purposes in the *marketable securities* account. In this way the funds could be kept working at interest and not lying fallow in the cash account. If on the other hand the firm's management expresses a personal propensity to play it safe, it may decide to keep such balances (i.e., gradually accumulate such balances) in its cash account. But if it chooses the latter course, it must add to the desired opening balance periodic (or occasional) amounts to accomplish this purpose (Figure 2-4).

Of course, if the firm elects this procedure it will incur an opportunity cost to the extent of lost interest. But if the firm is quite small and feels it is preempted from carrying marketable securities because of

---

[26] *Ibid.*, p. 423.
[27] *Ibid.*, p. 420.

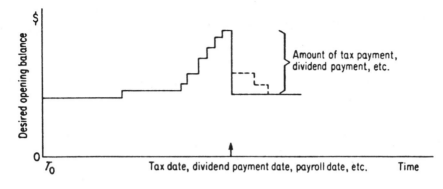

Figure 2-4. Illustration of how the "desired opening balance" could be increased for various purposes.

minimum purchase requirements, or because it cannot leave the balance on deposit at a savings and loan or commercial bank for the minimum period on which interest is paid, or simply because of the aforementioned problem of interest earned versus purchase cost, it may elect this course of action.

Before continuing to the next section, and to anticipate the perceptive reader who questions the possibility of *successive* negative changes in the cash account, it is well to add here that this is a factor in the determination of the optimal marketable securities account, and not the cash account. The presumption here is that if the opening balance is not up to the desired opening balance (within the constraints of the "indifference band") on any given day, the firm will sell marketable securities and that day bolster its balance up to the desired opening balance.[28]

DETERMINING THE OPTIMAL BALANCE FOR PAYROLL AND DIVIDEND SUBACCOUNTS

Many firms have found it convenient to maintain, in addition to their general (cash) account, subordinate accounts to service their payroll and dividend checks. Assuming such accounts, it is possible to devise a probabilistic model to assist in the management of such accounts.

The basic principle operative in these cases is the same as in the

---

[28]While the models set forth here are predicated on time intervals of one day, expansion to some other longer time interval might be accommodated. Again, this seems to turn on the relationship and agreement the firm has with its bank.

preceding treatment: the debits (withdrawals) made to such an account can be depicted by a probability distribution, and the use of such a distribution will provide the decision rule on how much to have in the account at any given point in time. But unlike the former model, the assumption of "independent trials" is quite tenuous. What happens the first day after a payroll is issued has a pronounced effect on what happens the second day, and the second day's activity affects the third, and so on. Thus the model presented here must be construed as only a first approximation to the solution. If the dollar volume involved warranted extensive analysis, the approach that seems to be most promising is a computerized simulation of the account utilizing a Markov chain process of conditional probabilities.

Barring a state law to the contrary, a firm that issues a given amount of payroll or dividend checks on, say, Friday need not have *that* amount in the account on *Friday*. In fact, not all the checks will be presented for payment to the firm's bank on Monday. If presented to another bank on Monday, it may be Tuesday before the check clears the firm's bank— possibly longer in the case of dividend checks, as there is a more pronounced float situation with respect to such checks. The latter case assumes, of course, more geographic distribution of the recipients of dividend checks than of payroll checks. But if a firm does not have to have the amount of the total payroll (or total dividend) on deposit immediately after issuance, how much should it have? The model (Figure 2-5) will illustrate this, but since it is a probabilistic decision, the same *caveat* as earlier applies: what chance is the firm willing to take of not having enough?

To help reach a decision rule on how much to have on deposit on the first (business) day after issuance of the checks (what ever day that might be), it should be useful to examine the experience of this account over time—say, the past three to five years. Assuming that there are not serious factors at work tending to change the pattern at least for the near future, a study of the recent past should be quite sufficient for near-term forecasting. Having constructed such a distribution for the first day (and Monday was used in the illustration), a decision rule can be chosen for the desired amount to be held on the first day, *given the risk* assumed. This process can then be repeated for each successive day until a new payroll date is reached: for example, there would be ten such distributions if the firm paid its employees every two weeks. Each successive distribution would be like the first, except that its modal value probably would be centered over a lower percentage-of-payroll figure, and

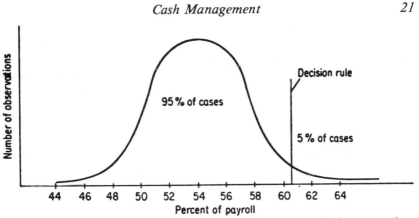

Figure 2-5. Frequency Distribution of the percent of total payroll checks presented for payment to a firm's bank on Monday, last five years.

presumably each successive decision rule (desired balance) would be smaller.

Once these respective distributions have been plotted and decision rules reached for each day in the interpayroll period, a model can then be constructed which will depict the desired dollar amount to be held for the whole period. Figure 2-6 illustrates such a composite (but naive) model.

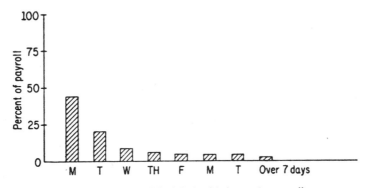

Figure 2-6. Composite model of desired balances in payroll account for period following issuance of check.

As previously mentioned, this same type of model could be constructed for a dividend account. In either case the reason for constructing such a model is the same: to keep funds invested in interest-earning assets as long as possible. While the firm would only be keeping some of their funds working a day or two or three longer, if this process were *repeated*

52 times a year (assuming a weekly payroll) it would amount to keeping, say 20–40 percent of their total payroll (or dividend payment) earning interest for 50–150 days a year. If the amounts involved are in the order of tens of millions of dollars, the interest earned will help pay the expense of the treasurer and his staff. If the amounts are smaller, the returns will be smaller, but it would still add to the firm's profit.

While on the subject of the firm's payroll it may be well at this point to remember that the longer the pay period, the greater the credit extended to the firm by the employees. In the past century daily pay was not uncommon, and even up to World War II weekly pay was the rule for most plants. It was in the early postwar period that checks were first widely used in paying employees. Were it not for the use of checks, and the fact that often many if not most of the employees have checking accounts at other banks, the preceding model would not be possible.[29]

Recently it was brought to the writer's attention that a firm's bank had worked out an innovation to assist a firm in handling its payroll account. No longer did the firm have to issue thousands of checks to its employees. Instead, it could transfer one sum from its general account, and the bank would set up individual accounts for *all* the employees. Each employee then had one "free" check per pay period. In this way, he could write a check for the amount of his pay and deposit it with his bank, or—and, in part this is what the bank hoped—he would use this account as his regular checking account. What the bank was trying to do obviously was the same thing suggested above for the business firm. It had the use of the unexpended balance until it was completely drawn down—and many new customers in addition! On the other hand, the firm gained the advantage of not issuing all the payroll checks, but it lost the interest that could be earned on the amounts in question. Since this firm had automated equipment for producing the checks, the cost would be rather low, but since the payroll amounted to millions of dollars, the small cost savings should have been overshadowed by the interest income foregone.[30]

---

[29]Not only would the interest income be lost, but the firm would have to incur substantial expense in filling the pay envelopes for all employees. It is a wonder that some firms still pay in currency, and weekly at that.

[30]In California there is an interesting state law that prescribes that employers *must* pay employees at least every 26 days. Also, another California law states that in the case of termination an employee must be paid the balance of the amount in the original offer of employment. If that is monthly, and termination takes place on the first day of a new month, then a whole month's pay must be given to the employee. Such a law as this obviously mediates against stretching the pay period too far.

DETERMINING THE OPTIMUM BALANCE IN THE MARKETABLE SECURITIES ACCOUNT

As previously stated, the purpose of maintaining a marketable-securities account as here defined is that it acts as a reserve for the cash account. When the cash account needs funds, because the daily opening balance is less than the desired opening balance, some securities are quickly sold and the cash account bolstered accordingly. If there is redundant cash (i.e., if the opening balance is above the upper limit of the indifference band) then securities can be purchased with the redundancy.

Within this frame of reference, therefore, some optimum balance of marketable securities should be carried to take care of the probable deficiencies in the cash account, but above this amount the marketable securities thus become redundant for the purpose at hand.

Before pursuing this matter further, let us remember that there are other purposes for holding marketable securities. As mentioned in the section on cash-balance determination, funds must be provided for meeting the controllable (known) outflows such as taxes and dividends. The accumulation of these outflows would thus cause the marketable securities account to rise above the desired daily level. And as the model to be formulated below will show, it is important that these funds be held *in addition* to the balance held for the primary purpose. This is so because it is entirely possible (but not "probable") that the day a large tax payment is due, for example, would be just the day when the cash balance took a maximum downturn.

If more marketable securities (defined as "free" marketable securities) are present in the firm's account than needed (i) to service the cash account, and (ii) to accommodate the controllable outlays then this excess amount would be available for financing other assets in the firm, e.g., receivables, inventory, and fixed assets. Of course if the firm does not have any immediate use for the funds in such other assets, it is better to keep these funds in marketable securities than in the cash account. But in this way a financial manager at least *knows* what his "free" balance of marketable securities is, and can act accordingly. If he does not estimate his needs, he may deny more profitable "other" investments—suffering in the process an opportunity cost. On the other hand, he may think he has more "free" marketable securities than he does and approve commitments that would require the liquidation of marketable securities. Here the opportunity cost may be the interest forgone and the interest incurred *if* he finds he needs the marketable securities that he unwisely sold.

Let us return now to the immediate question, How can a firm determine how much to hold in its marketable securities account for the primary purpose—i.e., the optimal (desired) balance? Having set up the model for the cash balance the approach to the solution to this question is at first easy, but becomes more complicated as it is made dynamic.

If all we were to consider was a *one-period* (e.g., one-day) analysis, the answer to how much marketable securities would be simply enough to cover the accepted maximum probable deficit in the cash account, or in other words, it would *equal* the opening balance. If the desired opening balance were set (on the basis of Figure 2-3) at say, $1,000,000, then this would be the amount of the (basic) optimal balance in the marketable securities account. The reason, of course, is that management has determined this to be the maximum decrease for which they are going to provide. If in those few cases the marketable securities account were insufficient to cover the daily decrease, then the logical alternative would be to borrow—for example, through a short-term loan. But if the firm does not have some sort of automatic loan arrangement[31] it would involve some trouble and effort to take out such loans frequently, and furthermore it may cause a deterioriation in rapport and relationship with the bank. Such frequent borrowing would be necessary, however, if the firm forgets that it is possible to have *successive* decreases *in the short run* of various amounts just through what we have called random events. Furthermore, as will subsequently be discussed, if the firm is expanding or contracting sales volume to any appreciable extent, it will introduce into the system a force that is not provided for. In this case estimates of the future flows should be made using accounts receivables as a regressor with sales, and "cash sales" (if material) as a regressor with sales; an estimate of accounts payable can be made by regressing this account with the estimated cost-of-goods-sold account.

Referring only to a short-run analysis, however, a probabilistic approach (Table 2-1) can be used to help determine the expected drain that would be put on the marketable securities account if successive maximum probable decreases were experienced.[32]

While $1,000,000 is the illustrative maximum probable decrease, it is unrealistic merely to double this to take account of two successive de-

---

[31]Such as an overdraft arrangement, or a line of credit they can draw upon at will.
[32]As in the case of the payroll model, an alternative approach to the model that follows is to devise a simulation model utilizing a Markov chain process. In fact, the matrix approach used in Markov chains is quite similar to the chain used here. The situation here, however, is rather unlike the preceding discussion regarding the conditional probabilities in the paryroll model. *Less* autocorrelation is assumed here.

Table 2-1. Computation of the Summation of Successive Maximum Probable Decreases Assuming $1,000,000 as Desired Opening Balance

		(1) Maximum Decrease in d_m	(2) Probability of Successive Decreases	Summation of Successive Decreases (1) × (2)
Starting value,	t_0	$1,000,000	1.00	$1,000,000
Expected value,	t_1	1,000,000	.50	500,000
	t_2	1,000,000	$.50^2$	250,000
	t_3	1,000,000	$.50^3$	125,000
	t_4	1,000,000	$.50^4$	62,500
	t_5	1,000,000	$.50^5$	31,250
	t_6	1,000,000	$.50^6$	15,630
	t_7	1,000,000	$.50^7$	7,810
	t_8	1,000,000	$.50^8$	3,910
	.	.	.	.
	.	.	.	.
	.	.	.	.
	t_{15}	1,000,000	$.50^{15}$	20
		Present value of successive decreases =		$1,996,100

creases, etc. This is so because we must consider the probability of two successive decreases. If the probability of a decrease (any decrease) is p — .5, then to the $1,000,000 a firm holds to take care of the first day (t_0) maximum decrease we must add $1,000,000 (.5) to take account of a decrease in day t_1. To take account of a whole chain of successive decreases, we would have to continue the process. Symbolically, if d_m is the maximum probable decrease, and m_0 is the optimal marketable securities balance, then

$$m_o = d_m + \sum_{i=1}^{i=n} d_m p^i, \qquad p = .50 \qquad (2\text{-}4)$$

Notice that the d_m used in this case was $1,000,000, the maximum probable decrease, and not the "expected" decrease.[33] This was done because of the express concern for successive *maximum* probable decreases. The weighted average decrease thus has little meaning here

[33]The expected decrease could be determined by an "expected-gain" model in which Figure 2-2 would be redrawn with the horizontal axis segregated into $200,000 increments. The area under the curve for each increment would be the probability of that change (and here we would be concerned only with a decrease). Taking a weighted average of all such decrements (with the probability of that decrement as the respective weights) would be the average expected decrease. In the illustration at hand, and assuming weights, respectively, of $p = .12$, $p = .08$, $p = .05$, and $p = .03$ plus $p = .02$ for an all-over $1,000,000 decrease, the expected decrease would be $226,000.

except to remind us that if we have a decrease it will probably be quite a lot less than $1,000,000. In other words, most of the day-to-day changes will be fairly close to the modal point of the distribution, and zero was assumed to be the modal value here. For the illustration at hand, therefore, the optimal balance of marketable securities, m_0, would be approximately $2,000,000.

While a "normal" distribution with the mode = 0 was used in the preceding illustration, the reader is cautioned against assuming a normal distribution with the mode = 0. If the firm is in the course of expanding, the distribution of the changes in the cash account probably would be skewed to the right, as in Figure 2-7, with the mode centered over some negative change.

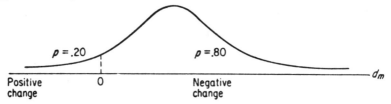

Figure 2-7. Illustrative distribution of daily changes in cash account (d_m), assuming expanding sales.

If the firm's sales are not expanding but retrenching, the distribution of d_m would probably be as depicted in Figure 2-8.

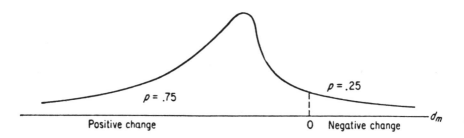

Figure 2-8. Illustrative distribution of daily changes in cash account (d_m), assuming contracting sales.

Now the purpose of Figures 2-7 and 2-8 is to remind the reader that the probability coefficient used in determining m_0, i.e., p in Eq. 2-4 and column (2) in Table 2-1, will be determined by each respective distribution of d_m. If, for example, $p > .50$, then $m_0 > $2,000,000$ for the assumed

$1,000,000 maximum decrease. Conversely, if the area in the "negative" tail of the d_m distribution is less than $p = .50$, then $m_0 < \$2,000,000$.

Determination of Free Marketable Securities

As noted earlier, one of the important by-products of the determination of the m_0 balance is that it assists in the determination of the firm's free (i.e., available) marketable securities. To determine the amount of free marketable securities, we must add to m_0 the amount of marketable securities held for the controllable outflows (m_c). Using m_f as the amount of free marketable securities, and M as the total marketable securities held, then

$$m_f = M - (m_0 + m_c). \qquad (2\text{-}5)$$

Summary

In this chapter the problem of "cash management" was decomposed into two basic areas: (i) a determination of the optimal cash balance, and once this was done, (ii) a determination of the optimal balance for marketable securities. The payroll and dividend models were treated together owing to their similarities, but the determination of the optimal daily balance following issuance of the checks was not necessary in the determination of the other two major models. The problem of providing for the requisite tax, payroll, dividend and other controllable amounts was considered a subset of the marketable securities account. Unlike Beranek's functions, it was shown that the logical optimal level of marketable securities depended on the maximum expected change in the cash account and not on the "returns from marketable securities."

Summarizing the models in symbolic form, the first determination is the maximum expected change in the cash account, d_m, given the probability p management is willing to accept of not having enough cash:

$$f(d_m) = 1 - p, \qquad p \ given \qquad (2\text{-}6)$$

Having determing d_m for a single period, the next problem is to take account of successive maximum probable decreases in order to determine the optimal amount of marketable securities, m_0:

$$m_0 = d_m + \sum_{i=1}^{i=n} d_m p^i \qquad (2\text{-}4)$$

where $p = .50$ as an example.

To determine the total required amount of marketable securities,

m', the firm must add to m_0 the amount accumulated for such controllable purposes as tax dates (x_t), payroll dates (w_t), dividend dates (I_t), and so forth. Thus:

$$m' = m_0 + m_c \qquad (2\text{-}7)$$

where

$$m_c = f(x_t, w_t, I_t, \ldots, N_t) \qquad (2\text{-}8)$$

If the firm wishes to determine "how much" of its marketable securities are free for investment elsewhere (usually in the firm), it may do so by the following:

$$m_f = M - (m_0 + m_c). \qquad (2\text{-}5)$$

SUGGESTED READINGS

Archer, Stephen H., "A Model for the Determination of Firm Cash Holdings," *Journal of Financial and Quantitative Analysis,* March 1966, pp. 1–10 (discussion by Virginia McKennie-Belt, pp. 11–14).

Baumol, William J., "The Transaction Demand for Cash: An Inventory Theoretic Approach," *Quarterly Journal of Economics,* November 1952, pp. 545–556.

Beranek, William, *Analysis for Financial Decisions* (Homewood, Ill.: Irwin 1963), Chap. 11, pp. 345–391.

Bierman, Harold, Jr., and Alan K. McAdams, *Management Decisions for Cash and Marketable Securities,* Cornell Studies in Policy and Administration (Ithaca, N.Y.: Cornell Graduate School of Business and Public Administration, 1962).

Hicks, John R., "Mr. Keynes and the 'Classics': A Suggested Interpretation," *Econometrica,* April 1937, pp. 147–159.

Keynes, John Maynard, "Alternative Theories of the Rate of Interest," *Economic Journal,* June 1937, pp. 241–252.

———, *The General Theory of Employment, Interest and Money* (New York: Harcourt, 1935), Chap. 13 and 15.

Miller, Merton H., and Daniel Orr, "A Model of the Demand for Money by Firms," Report 6601, Center for Mathematical Studies in Business and Economics, University of Chicago. Also appeared in the *Quarterly Journal of Economics,* August 1966, pp. 413–435. Contains a good bibliography.

———, "An Application of Control-Limit Models to the Management of Corporate Cash Balances," in *Proceedings of the Conference on Financial Research and Its Implications for Management* (Stanford, Calif.: Stanford U. P., 1966).

Stancill, James McN., Jr., "The Determination of Corporate Holdings of Cash and Marketable Securities," in Edward J. Mock (ed.), *Financial Decision-Making* (Scranton, Pa.: International Textbook, 1967).

APPENDIX

REDUCTION OF FLOAT: A LOCKBOX MODEL*

With firms doing more business nationally, the problem of float has expanded. *Float* is the term for the dollar amount of checks that a firm could cash were they not in the mail. If firm A mails a check to firm B, that check, until it is cashed, represents what might be called *desirable* float to firm A, but *undesirable* float to firm B. The check that firm A has written will not have to be covered while it is *en route* to B, or while it is being cleared through the banking system. If firm A is on the East Coast and firm B on the West Coast, as much as four days could elapse for mail transmittal, and another three to four days for clearance of the check through the banking system. While this is advantageous to firm A (the maker of the check), it is "sterile" money to firm B. If the check is for an invoice to firm B, then B, presumably, could take certain steps to reduce this undesirable float.

The most popular technique developed recently to reduce float is the use of what is called a *lockbox*. A lockbox is merely a post office box in a distant city. A local bank in that city or a branch of the firm's bank, can be given authority to open the mail received through the lockbox, process the checks and daily, or otherwise, transfer the funds so received to the principal bank account of the firm. This transfer is usually made via telegraphic means. Thus if firm A were in Los Angeles and firm B's bank in New York, then firm B could specify that the check be mailed to a post office box in Los Angeles. With the improved local mail handling (ABC delivery) the check could be in B's lockbox the night it was mailed. If the check is drawn on the bank administering the lockbox arrangement, then it is possible for the amount of the check to be transferred to B's New York bank the next day. In this case, therefore, B would have the amount of the check at its disposal six to eight days sooner than if it had followed conventional methods.

Another way of viewing the reduction of float to firm B is as a reduction in accounts receivable. For some firms, the *mean* period for an account receivable to be outstanding might be in the order of fifteen to

*This Appendix originally appeared as "A Lock-Box Model" in *Management Science*, Vol. 15, No. 2 (October 1968), pp. B-84–87.

eighteen days.[1] If three to six days could be subtracted from this period, then the investment in accounts receivable could be reduced by 10–20 percent.

With the increasing tightness of capital in recent years, firms are turning to ways of freeing funds for operating purposes. Until Ferdinand K. Levy's paper[2] in 1966 the subject of lockbox management was apparently untouched in the journals. Levy's model assumes a given body of accounts receivable, and thus a fixed potential for revenue from lockboxes. From this framework he develops a system for the ordering of the selection of lockbox sites. Levy does not direct his paper to whether or not a lockbox should be established, however, and it is to this question, principally, that this comment is directed.

THE DECISION TO ESTABLISH A LOCKBOX

Essentially the decision to establish a lockbox is based on the yield that could be realized on the freed funds *vis-à-vis* the cost of the arrangement. In the delineation of the variables in the decision rule that is suggested in this appendix, yield must be defined as the opportunity cost (or income) of the amount of funds made available through the lockbox. This becomes a little complicated in a generalized decision rule because the firm in question may be a net borrower or a net investor. If the firm is borrowing, on balance, to finance its working capital (implying no free marketable securities), then the opportunity cost of the funds unnecessarily tied up in float would be the firm's marginal borrowing rate. In some cases, for example, those in which the receivables have to be factored to provide operating cash, this might mean an opportunity cost of 12–20 percent per year (before tax). If the firm is borrowing from a bank at 6–10 percent interest, then a reduction in the receivable balance could mean a reduction in the loan balance outstanding. Thus the opportunity cost here would be the 6–10 percent (before tax) interest that would otherwise be paid.

On the other hand, if the reduction in the investment in receivables would mean a greater free marketable securities balance, then the opportunity cost might be 4–5 percent (before taxes). In other words, by *not*

---

[1]Based on the assumption that the cash discount period is 10 days and the credit period 30 days.

[2]Ferdinand K. Levy "An Application of Heuristic Problem Solving to Accounts Receivable Management," *Management Science,* Vol. 12, No. 6 (February 1966), pp. B-236–B-244.

being able to invest in marketable securities in the amount of the un-desired float, then an opportunity income of 4–5 percent per year (before taxes) on this amount is lost.

It might be argued that the yield should be figured as the firm's so-called "cost of capital," but I feel this would be in error, even if a realistic figure could be derived for the firm's cost of capital. If the reader wishes to consider this opportunity cost, defined as *i*, as the appropriate rate for the firm in question, however, the substance of the model will not be altered in any way.

The *new* float period will be defined as t_1; the *former* float period will be t_2. The yearly dollar volume of credit sales in the given area will be defined as V. T will be the applicable corporate income tax rate.

On the cost side, the total number of items, i.e., checks sent to the lockbox yearly, will be defined as *H*. The cost for processing these items, unless a yearly flat fee (*F*) is charged, are: (1) the handling fee (*h*)—a charge of, usually, 2–7 cents per item; (2) the check cashing fee (*c*), usually about 10–15 cents per item, and (3) the wire transfer cost (*w*), while *W* is the total number of wire transfers per year—probably a little less than $52 \times 5 = 260$. If a minimum balance (*M*) must be maintained as a condition of the lockbox, then the after tax opportunity cost of this, too, represents a cost. If, however, the bank is willing to provide another service in addition to the lockbox, in return for the minimum balance, then this benefit should be explicitly cited in the "benefit" (left-hand) side of the equation, or as a subtraction from *M*, tax adjusted of course.

THE LOCKBOX DECISION RULE

Once the respective variables in the equation have been delineated, the decision to effect a lockbox in a given area may be determined from the following decision rule, expressed as an inequality: Secure a lockbox if

$$\frac{V}{360} \cdot (t_2 - t_1) \cdot i(1 - T) \gtreqless [H(h + c) + Ww](1 - T) + M[i(1 - T)]$$

$$(\text{2A-1})$$

If a flat fee (*F*) is charged in lieu of the per-item costs, then in order for the bank to receive the same compensation, the fee would have to be

$$F(1 - T) = [H(h + c) + Ww](1 - T) + M[i(1 - T)] \qquad (\text{2A-2})$$

As an aside, if a flat fee is charged, there is usually no compensating balance requirement.

Equation (2A-1) could then be expressed as

$$\frac{V}{360} \cdot (t_2 - t_1) \cdot i (1 - T) \geqq F(1 - T) \qquad (2A\text{-}3)$$

EXAMPLE OF THE DECISION RULE

Suppose a firm in New York does business with firms in the greater Los Angeles area, and the following values[3] for the variables hold:

$$V = \$18,000,000 \text{ per year}$$
$$t_2 = 9 \text{ days}$$
$$t_1 = 3 \text{ days}$$
$$i = .08$$
$$T = .50$$
$$H = 3,000 \text{ items per year (expected)}$$
$$h = \$0.04$$
$$c = \$0.12$$
$$W = 260$$
$$w = \$3$$
$$M = \$60 \text{ per item} = \$180,000$$

Substituting these values into Eq. (2A-1), yields

$$\frac{18,000,000}{360} \cdot (9 - 3) \cdot .08(.50)$$
$$\geqq [3000(.04 + .12) + 260(3)](1 - .50) + 180,000[.08(1 - .50)]$$

and

$$[50,000 \times 6] \cdot (.04) \geqq 48 , + 780 + 7200$$

which solves to

$$\$12,000 \geqq \$8,460$$

Thus a net profit after tax of \$3,540 could be realized by utilizing a lockbox in Los Angeles, with the variables as specified.

LOCATING LOCKBOXES

Since the above decision rule is a generalized model for the decision to establish a lockbox, then it follows that the location of lockboxes is

[3]The costs used in this example were adopted from the practice of a Los Angeles bank. These charges may differ in other cities and are intended to be only illustrative.

simply a function of the decision rule for each potential site. If ordering the sequence of lockbox locations is of any moment, then the ranking should be according to the greatest *profit* realized, and not the *least cost* of any potential individual lockbox arrangement.[4]

EXPERIENCE WITH LOCKBOXES

According to a recent survey[5] a growing number of firms are utilizing the lockbox services of banks. The experience of many firms was good, but a number of firms reported that they were having trouble with some of their customers who insisted on mailing (*via* regular mail of course!) their checks and invoices to the main office instead of the lockbox (*i.e.*, post office box) in their area. Naturally, whether the firm tolerates this practice or not depends on the respective bargaining strength of the parties.

A side benefit with lockbox arrangements is that if the firm needs banking facilities in a distant city (because of expansion, for example) they have already-established rapport with a (suitable) bank.

Firms anticipating using a lockbox must remember, however, that they should not anticipate any significant reduction in paper work as a result of such an arrangement. True, they will be spared making the deposit of the checks involved, but all of the invoices must still be processed after receipt from the lockbox administrator. Furthermore, it is standard practice that if the administrator-bank receives any irregular items, such as a check written against an invoice for a lesser amount and marked "paid in full" the whole package—check and invoice—will be mailed to the firm. Also, a certain amount of correspondence and long-distance phoning must be anticipated.

[4]The "least-cost" approach is taken for the selection of a lockbox location from among *n* possible sites by Levy. Levy's paper was directed to the optimum location (or ranking) of lockboxes, and since he assumed a constant revenue, a least-cost approach is tenable. In a generalized model, however, it is necessary to take account of varying revenues and costs and thus the necessity for ranking by maximum profit instead of least cost.

[5]Edward J. Mock and Donald Schuckett, "Increasing the Velocity of Corporate Funds," *Management Services*, July-August 1966, pp. 39–47.

CHAPTER 3

Management of the Marketable Securities Portfolio

In Chapter 2 a firm's total holdings of marketable securities M were divided into securities to service the cash account m_0, securities held to meet controllable (known) cash outflows m_c and the balance of securities held in the portfolio and identified as free marketable securities m_f. Thus

$$M = m_0 + m_c + m_f \qquad (3\text{-}1)$$

In this chapter the topical areas to be discussed are (1) the identification of the variables and risks to be encountered in the decision-making process of security selection; (2) the determining of which securities are appropriate for inclusion in each part of the portfolio M; and (3) the mechanics of the purchase and sale of money-market instruments (securities).

VARIABLES IN MARKETABLE SECURITIES SELECTION

When a portfolio manager selects a security from among the spectrum of those offered in the market, he presumably does so by careful evaluation of the relevant variables indigenous to such securities. These variables are the safety, marketability, and yield of the security. Additionally, the purchase of a security also assumes the assumption of certain associated risks. Some of these risks are indigenous to the security per se, and some are exogenous and therefore outside of the control of the portfolio manager. Thus it is necessary to discuss not only the variables, but the risks associated with the variables.

Safety

Safety in a marketable security is the term used to connote the probability of partial or total loss of principal. Since debt instruments, as opposed to stock certificates, are promises to repay a stipulated sum of money at the maturity of the instrument, the safety of that instrument (*i.e.*, promise to pay) is the probability function that the debt will be paid. Thus the safety of an obligation of the U.S. government is as close to certainty as it is possible to get simply because the government could, if it wished, merely print the money (legal tender) that it requires to pay off the debt. Debt instruments issued by business firms and state and local governments perforce do not have this degree of safety. Instead, safety in this connection implies inability to repay at maturity.

As discussed below, high safety is the very essence of money-market instruments.[1] This is so not only because short-term treasuries are included, but because the safety of an issue must be unquestioned to be included in a dealer's money-market instruments inventory. The short-term nature of a debt instrument is not sufficient to make it a money-market instrument, but, coupled with impeccable safety, it *could* be a money-market instrument.

Marketability

While it is possible that a security could be quite "safe," this does not imply that it is possible to sell the security *before* maturity without loss. Thus the marketability of all securities is a function of the so-called breadth and depth of the market for such securities. While *breadth* is a rather nebulous term, it generally refers to the number of participants in the market and, to a lesser extent, is suggestive of the geographic dispersion of the market. *Depth*, on the other hand, refers to the ability of the market, no matter how narrow or broad, to absorb the purchase or sale of *substantial* dollar amounts of securities.

For money-market instruments—which are the main topic of this chapter—there is sufficient depth, generally, but there is not the breadth that may be desired. Breadth, however, is usually not as critically necessary as depth for money-market instruments. Long-distance telephone calls can take care of distance problems. When the market for a security

---

[1]Money-market instruments consist of short-term issues (or long-term issues that are within a year or so of maturity) of the U.S. Treasury and certain other short-term issues of debt, e.g., certificates of deposit, repurchase agreements, commercial paper and bankers' acceptances. Each of these will be specifically discussed below.

lacks both depth and breadth, however, the holder of such security is said to be "locked in"; the holder may be able to sell his securities to a dealer but the implication of a sale at a loss is quite clear.

Yield

The yield on a debt instrument is simply the interest and/or appreciation of principal. Some securities, notably Treasury bills, do not pay "interest" as such, instead they are sold at "discount," with the face amount due at maturity. Thus a $10,000 bill might be purchased for $9,800. In this case the yield of $200 would be expressed in terms of an equivalent yearly interest-rate percentage, e.g., 6 percent.

RISKS IN MARKETABLE SECURITIES

Risk of Safety

Aside from U.S. Treasury securities, whose safety is considered certain, the indication of the safety of a security varies with its maker and type.[2] Bonds are graded as to safety by at least two major services— Moody's and Standard and Poor's Investment Service. Moody's Aaa is the top rank for a bond and indicates impeccable safety, e.g., the bonds of A.T. & T. or General Motors. Unfortunately there is no equivalent grading of money-market instruments. Instead, there is a screening process performed by every dealer of such securities. This is not to say, however, that securities of questionable safety do not enter the money market, for in fact they do. Several banks that collapsed in recent years had outstanding negotiable certificates of deposit (CD's). But the percentage of such securities in the total dollar volume of money-market securities is quite small.

To invade the commercial paper market, for example, a firm would usually have to have already established its financial strength and viability, say, in the corporate bond market. Even then, to be generally accepted by the dealers a firm should also be well known in the popular sense. But if sheer asset size is the major determinant—or discriminant—of safety, the buyer must be aware of what he is buying. According to the National Credit Office in New York City,[3] about 60 percent of

---

[2]Stocks—preferred and common—are excluded from this discussion since safety, in the context used here, refers to the probability of repayment of a debt at maturity.

[3]Cited in *Money Market Instruments*, 2d ed. (Cleveland: Federal Reserve Bank of Cleveland, 1965, p. 43.)

firms issuing commercial paper had net worth of $25 million or less. (Table 3-1.)

Marketability Risk

Because the marketability of a security is difficult to even define, it follows that any attempt to appraise the risk associated with the marketability of a security is, *a fortiori*, difficult to define. Virtually all securities susceptible of inclusion in the m_0 and m_c portfolio (discussed subsequently), have a well-established secondary market,[4] with commercial

TABLE 3-1   **Net Worth of Commercial Paper Borrowers**

Firms with net worth of:	1955	1960	1963
Over $25 million	19.4	32.7	41.6
$5 to 25 million	34.8	37.0	39.9
$1 to 5 million	42.9	28.5	18.0
Less than $1 million	2.9	1.8	0.5
	100.0	100.0	100.0

Source: National Credit Office, New York, as cited in *Money Market Instruments,* p. 43.

paper a possible exception. The better established the secondary market, *ceteris paribus,* the lower the marketability risk. This secondary market may take different forms for different types of securities. In some cases dealers "make" a market by offering to buy and sell generic types of securities. In other cases—for example, the market for federal funds— one or two firms in New York act as a "floor post," where offers to buy and sell are matched against each other.

Yield Risks

Even if there is a substantial secondary market (implying that capital loss should not be attributed mainly to lack of breadth or depth) the resale of a security before maturity may result in a material loss owing to what is called the interest-rate risk. Since the price of a security acts inversely to the yield on that security to maturity, if interest rates (or yield) on a certain type of security, or for that class of securities, goes up, then the market price goes down. When prices in a securities market, such as the money market, appear to be getting volatile, a portfolio manager may try to avoid sale of securities before maturity, or hedge such possibility by

---

[4]A secondary market is essentially a secondhand market, meaning, of course, that securities after issuance may be freely traded. The best known example of a secondary market is the New York Stock Exchange.

setting up a repurchase agreement with a dealer. Under the latter arrangement, the firm may effect the resale of securities to the dealer for a previously agreed-upon price.[5] Of course, this is not a one-way street, and if a firm wishes to hedge against interest-rate or marketability risk, it must pay a price.

Measurement of the Risk

If a security is purchased at a price to yield a certain percent to maturity and, in fact, the security is held to maturity, then a payoff of the principal (plus interest en route, if any) will effect the yield originally calculated. In this case the yield risk is the safety risk. The allusion to yield risk in the preceding section, however, is to the probability function of the expected yield on a security if sold prior to maturity.

In the latter context, then, the expected yield (μ) is the mean of a (subjective) probability distribution with a variance, σ^2. Thus if a portfolio manager is acting rationally, he will attempt to maximize expected yield for a given variance; or, for a given expected yield, he will attempt to select a security with the lowest variance.

The problem is not just the selection of a low risk (*i.e.*, low relative variance) security, but the composition of a portfolio which will embody the desired yield, within the variance constraint or vice versa. Harry Markowitz, in a path-breaking article[6] in 1952, defined such a portfolio as an "efficient portfolio," and demonstrated the possibility of a portfolio of securities with a variance in expected rate of return (yield) that was smaller than the variance of any included securities.

Stimulated by the Markowitz article, and a subsequent monograph[7] others have added effectively to the matter of yield risk and portfolio selection. Working from a utility-function approach and utilizing factor analysis of the variance and covariance coefficients of the expected yield of a security, Donald Farrar[8] has demonstrated that a whole series of optimum (*i.e.*, "efficient" in the Markowitz sense) portfolios may be produced by solving a quadratic programming problem using a series of

---

[5]As discussed below, repurchase agreements are a form of money-market instruments and thus a medium in themselves. Repurchase agreement, as used here, implies convenience to the firm holding a security, and not a means of borrowing, *per se*, for the dealer.

[6]H. Markowitz, "Portfolio Selection," *Journal of Finance* (March 1952).

[7]H. Markowitz, *Portfolio Selection: Efficient Diversification of Investments*, Cowles Foundation Monograph No. 16 (New York: Wiley, 1959).

[8]Donald Farrar, *The Investment Decision Under Uncertainty* (Englewood Cliffs, N.J.: Prentice-Hall, 1962).

"risk-aversion" coefficients. More recently, Mao and Sarndal[9] have developed an approach which, while drawing on the work of Markowitz, Farrar, and William Sharpe, is somewhat different from that mentioned above. Mao and Sarndal's approach is the determination of an optimal portfolio—with respect to yield risk—through the use of Bayesian probabilities with respect to the apparent future state of the market. Relative to this chapter and the money market, if one foresees an optimistic future (near-term) for the market, he can translate his feelings into an optimistic probability P and a pessimistic probability $Q = 1 - P$. Working from these estimates of the future market (probabilities of "states of nature"), it is now possible to construct a portfolio in the Farrar manner, but with explicit recognition of the expected state of the market.

While the above-mentioned writings on the problem of yield risk and portfolio selection are but a brief sketch of the work being done, and are not intended to be inclusive, they do point out the rather esoteric treatment the subject is receiving. For some managers of a marketable-securities portfolio, a mathematical approach to at least portions of their portfolio seems quite possible.

SELECTING SECURITIES FOR THE PORTFOLIO SEGMENTS

Trichotomizing the total portfolio M into m_0, m_c and m_f portions for the purposes mentioned in Chapter 2 is also convenient for the following discussion of which securities to select for inclusion in each segment. Basically, the securities that should be included in each segment are a function of the degree of speed needed to convert the security into cash. The m_0 portion needs securities that can be converted into cash quickly (*e.g.*, the same day as the sale). This is necessary owing to the assumptions and conditions precedent assumed by the cash model. The m_c portion, however, presumes that the conversion date is known, at least to within a day or two of the actual date. If funds are being earmarked for a bimonthly payroll, or a quarterly dividend or tax payment, this requirement permits the portfolio manager the flexibility of timing maturities or sales to meet a known demand for cash.

The free marketable securities segment m_f presents a situation quite different from both m_c and m_0 characteristics. While the date of conversion into cash is not known with certainty (like the m_0 situation), the need

[9]James C. T. Mao and Carl E. Sarndal, "A Decision Theory Approach to Portfolio Selection," *Management Science*, Vol. 12, No. 8 (April 1966), pp. B-323–333.

for quick conversion is not present. By definition, m_f contains those marketable securities which are free for investment elsewhere in the firm, for disbursement to stockholders, for voluntary retirement of debt or, possibly, for repurchase (and retirement) of the firm's own stock. Thus, given the nature of the possible demand for conversion of m_f securities into cash, it seems most probable that "regular-way" delivery (four days) of the proceeds of the sale of any or all included securities is quite compatible with the situation, the point of this argument being, therefore, that yield and not marketability should be the first criteria for selection with safety being second. Failure to make this three-part distinction in the character of the segments has cost—in yield lost—a number of firms. To some firms, marketable securities mean near-cash, irrespective of the prospective demands that will be placed on such holdings.[10]

In the following discussion, therefore, a description of the nature and risk characteristics of the securities that appear appropriate for each segment of the portfolio will be presented.

THE m_0 SEGMENT

Since the sole purpose of the m_0 segment of M is to service the cash account, the major requirement for any securities used to fund this segment must be readily and immediately convertible into cash.[11] The only money-market instrument that meets this criteria well is U.S. Treasury bills and other obligations of the U.S. Treasury that are maturing within one year. Collectively these securities are called the "floating debt" of the Treasury.[12]

THE m_c SEGMENT

Freed from the necessity of converting securities into cash (*i.e.*, a deposit at the firm's bank) the same day as the sale, there is greater variety

---

[10]It was precisely this distinction in demand that led the de' Medici family to great wealth in banking. By observing that bags of gold deposited with them were lying idle, fractional-reserve banking was born.

[11]If the bank the firm uses allows overdrafts of more than one day—a definite possibility in Canada, for example—then the assumption of same-day delivery of the proceeds of the securities sale may be relaxed. In this case many of the instruments listed as applicable for the m_c segment could be used for the m_0 segment.

[12]Currently, about $112 billion of the national debt is included in the floating-debt category. This term does not include maturing savings bonds, as these are not negotiable. Of the $112 billion, $72 billion represents Treasury bills, and the balance is maturing bonds, certificates, and notes.

of type of security for inclusion in the m_c segment of the portfolio. Furthermore, there is greater variety within the type of security selected. In general, there are five types of money-market instruments particularly adaptable to the m_c segment: commercial paper, negotiable certificates of deposit, bankers' acceptances, repurchase agreements and short-term securities of federal agencies.

Commercial Paper

Commercial paper is the popular terminology for the set of short-term credit instruments issued by corporations. Traditionally, commercial paper included paper issued by industrial, commercial, financial, and banking corporations. Of all the money-market instruments available, commercial paper is the oldest in this country, dating back to the early nineteenth century.

Being of a rather uniform legal character, commercial paper is the unsecured general obligation of the issuer, with a maturity of from about five days up to nine to twelve months.[13] The most popular maturities are from four to six months, with nine-month maturities also quite common. With the rise of direct placement of commercial paper, maturities are often tailored to mature on the day desired by the purchaser.

The size of the denomination of commercial paper varies with the issuer, but $25,000 would be about the minimum denomination. If purchased directly from the issuer, the note will be written for the desired amount, within the minimum denomination.

Commercial paper, like Treasury bills, may be sold at discount, meaning that the interest earned results in the difference between the purchase price and the face, or maturity, value of the note or it may earn interest at maturity.

About 40 percent of commercial paper is issued by manufacturing firms, about 30–35 percent by finance companies, and the balance by some well-known wholesalers, retailers, and others. Of the finance companies that issue such short-term paper, over half represents finance companies specializing in automobile-dealer financing. Small loan finance companies of substantial size, such as Beneficial Finance and

---

[13]It is possible to purchase commercial paper direct from the issuer with maturities as short as one day, but since it takes about four days for collection and deposit of funds via the regular way, such short-term paper involves special arrangements for collection. It is also possible to purchase commercial paper from a dealer with very short maturities, but this is rare and usually not done owing to the commission that must be paid. (See also the discussion regarding repurchase agreements below.)

Household Finance, account for most of the balance of finance-company paper.

While commercial paper may be purchased from dealers[14] in commercial paper, the period since World War II has seen the rapid increase in "direct placements." Instead of "shopping" dealers for the type of issuer and maturity desired, many firms have elected to call a firm of the type desired and arrange to purchase paper directly. This process saves the dealer commission (paid by the seller), approximately 10 to 25 "basis points,"[15] determined by the yearly equivalent interest yield on the paper. In early 1970 there was approximately $36 billion of commercial paper outstanding, of which about one-third was sold through dealers, the balance being placed directly. Less than 500 firms sell paper through dealers, and while practically all of these also sell directly, other firms sell their paper only via the direct route. This is so because dealers are very selective in the commercial paper they will take for resale. The dealers do not endorse the paper they handle, but the buyer does feel that the dealer gives his implicit approval of the issuer. An interesting feature of most commercial paper, incidentally, is a provision that permits the holder to present the note for payment, on an adjusted basis, if the financial condition of the issuer should substantially deteriorate. Failure to honor maturing commercial paper is almost nonexistent, so this feature is interesting but of little moment.

The selectivity of dealers also leads to a lack of breadth in the secondary market for commercial paper. If a holder wishes to dispose of commercial paper prior to maturity, he must find a dealer willing to purchase the paper, or, quite improbably, locate another firm that will buy the paper. If the paper was issued by a firm that does not meet the standards (size, financial condition and, quite importantly, reputation) of the dealer, then the holder of the paper is locked in, and must wait for maturity. With reluctance, the issuer might repurchase the paper. Firms should avoid requesting this, however. Another alternative is to pledge the paper as collateral for a bank loan, unless the firm is preempted from such borrowing. Even with the lowest-grade (and thus high yield) paper, the firm will find that there is at least a one percent disadvantage in the borrowing rate vis-à-vis the yield on the commercial paper pledged.

---

[14]In a subsequent section of this chapter, the principal dealers in commercial paper will be cited.

[15]A basis point is equal to one one-hundredth (1/100) of 1 percent. Thus 0.01   1 basis point.

Banker's Acceptances

By definition, a banker's acceptance is a time draft drawn on a bank, usually, by a foreign trader. In use in the United States only since 1913, when the Federal Reserve was established, banker's acceptances have been used in Europe for centuries.

Since it is not the purpose of this chapter to explore all of the intricacies of money-market instruments from the point of view of the issuer, a brief description of banker's acceptances will serve our purpose.

According to the regulations of the Federal Reserve System, there are only four types of banker's acceptances: bills to finance exports or imports, bills to finance the storage of goods in domestic and international trade, and bills of foreign exchange. In the first three cases, a banker's acceptance comes about thus: If an importer (in this country or abroad) buys merchandise, but does not have the funds to pay for the merchandise on the spot, he may finance the purchase by drawing a "bill" (*i.e.*, a standardized form of IOU) on his bank. If the bank accepts the bill, it will forward to the foreign exporter the price of the merchandise. The importer has thus borrowed the amount of the merchandise. At this point the bank has to choose between two courses of action. It may keep the bill as it would any note evidencing the indebtedness of any short-term loan, or it may sell the bill to a dealer on a discount basis. Prior to the sale of the bill to a dealer, the bill would be "two-name" paper, *i.e.*, the maker (the importer in this example) and the bank that accepted the bill. Once the dealer resells the paper, now called a banker's acceptance, it becomes "three-name" paper, with the dealer's name being the addition to the first two. It is readily seen, therefore, that with three firms legally responsible for payment of the banker's acceptance at maturity, the safety of the instrument is hardly questionable.

Banker's acceptances may also come about by the action of the exporter. If he receives an order for merchandise, he may make the draft to his favor, and then present it to a bank. Before accepting it, the bank would then arrange credit—directly or through the buyer's bank—for the amount and, accordingly, a banker's acceptance would thus be created. If goods are in international transit (which may take months) or in storage, a loan for all or part of the value of the goods may be secured, and a banker's acceptance is a common way of effecting this transaction. While of minor importance to the total volume of banker's acceptances, a foreign bank may secure the dollars to honor the payment to an American firm for goods bought by a foreign firm by borrowing dollars from an American bank, usually in New York—the intention being that at a later date the foreign bank will have the dollars to pay off the banker's acceptance it has created.

In brief form, therefore, the preceding discussion has shown how a banker's acceptance might come about in four different but related transactions. From the point of view of the manager of a marketable securities portfolio, however, it is quite immaterial why the banker's acceptance was created. He views the instrument as a quite safe negotiable money-market security with a yield slightly in excess of Treasury bills.

While a limited number of dealers[16] "make" the market for banker's acceptances the volume of banker's acceptances grew noticeably with the increase in world trade in the 1950's and 1960's. With the "credit crunch" of 1969, the outstanding amount of banker's acceptances held by firms other than banks and the Federal Reserve declined from about $2 billion (in 1967) to $1,495 billion at the end of June 1969.

The presence of the Federal Reserve in the market for three-name paper, incidentally, adds a stabilizing influence to the market. In seasonal periods of slow demand for banker's acceptances, the Federal Reserve has, traditionally, entered the market as a purchaser.

The secondary market for banker's acceptances is centered on a few (principally New York) dealers who make their profit by buying such paper at a price that would yield about 12½ basis points less than the current market yield, and reselling "at market."[17]

Maturities of Banker's acceptances are standardized (with some exceptions) at 90 days, although purchase of paper with less than 90 days to maturity is of course possible.

The yield differential on banker's acceptances vis-à-vis treasury bills has varied in the postwar period from as little as 20 basis points to as much as 50 or more basis points.

Certificates of Deposit

The newest instrument in the money market today is the negotiable certificate of deposit (CD). Prior to 1961, banks were permitted to issue negotiable certificates for a time deposit at the bank. Instead of issuing a familiar (nonnegotiable) passbook for the time deposit, the bank issued

---

[16]Examples of firms dealing in banker's acceptances are: M & T Discount Company, Merrill, Lynch, Pierce, Fenner & Smith, Inc., Bankers Discount Company, Discount Corporation of New York, and Briggs Schaedle & Company, Inc.

[17]This yield differential is of course subject to change owing to vagaries in the money market.

a "certificate," evidencing the amount and maturity of the indebtedness. But until the first part of 1961, very few banks did issue CD's. The ones that did were mainly outside the mainstream of financial activity. And the major banks would ask, Why should we? If we were to sell a money-market instrument, firms, mainly nonfinancial, industrial firms, would simply draw down their checking account to buy such a security. In short, for the whole period of low interest rates—the 1940's and 1950's in particular—why should a bank pay for money they got free?

With the secular rise in interest rates, especially short-term rates, many corporate treasurers started looking around for short-term investments. The banks soon found that firms were reducing their demand deposits in an effort to make these funds earn interest. The banks thus realized it was a question of offering an instrument of their own or losing funds to the established sectors of the money market. When the applicable Regulation Q of the Federal Reserve was modified to provide for competitive rates on CD's (over three months), the rush to sell this instrument was on.

From a very modest volume in 1962, CD's have become so popular that in January 1967, there was close to $18 billion outstanding. Indicative of the power and prestige of New York City banks is the fact that about $7 billion of the total represented indebtedness of banks in the nation's largest city. In mid-1969, however, the total declined to $13.5 billion, with $11.15 billion outside New York City.

Owing to the fact that the maximum permissible rate for CD's of less than 90-day maturity (typically only 1 percent) is not competitive in the money market, new CD's are issued with a minimum maturity of three months. But like other money-market instruments, shorter maturities represent no particular problem, since at least several dealers (including the Irving Trust Company, itself an issuer of CD's) make a rather active secondary market for the securities.

While the yield differential between CD's and Treasury bills is generally less than for prime commercial paper, the range in possible yields (*i.e.*, the "spread" between different quality paper) is rather significant —50 to 75 basis points. Three factors, principally, determine the difference in yield between one CD and another. First, of course, is the reputation (and size) of the issuing bank. The largest and best known sell for the lowest yield. But since there are over 300 banks with CD's outstanding, some of the issuers are considerably smaller and are not well known. Secondly, since CD's have become so popular, particularly with nonfinancial firms, CD's with maturities just before the popular tax payment dates will, *ceteris paribus*, have a slightly lower yield. Thirdly, the denomination of the CD is also a variable. The most popular denomination is $1 million. If a smaller denomination is desired, a very slight increase in yield (about 10 basis points) may be obtained.

Since the secondary market for CD's is quite deep, meaning that substantial holdings of CD's may be disposed of in one transaction, potential buyers are warned that disposal of small amounts of CD's may be a problem. Some dealers do not want to buy denominations of less than $500,000, and still others do not wish to purchase CD's of small or even middle-size banks. If a firm wishes to purchase CD's of the less desirable banks, therefore, it should time the maturities such that a quick sale in the secondary market is not necessary. It is possible, however, to effect a repurchase agreement with a dealer for CD's at the mutually agreed-upon yield (and price). If a firm buys lower-grade CD's and coincidentally establishes a repurchase agreement for a certain date, it may break even, considering the yield spread for the lower-grade paper less the price for the repurchase agreement. If skillfully done, the combination of a repurchase agreement and somewhat lower-grade paper may produce a net yield somewhat higher than the purchase of CD's with a very good secondary market. However, if a change in plans (or need) transpires, the firm may find itself locked-in by such maneuvering.

Unlike Treasury bills, commercial paper and banker's acceptances, CD's are sold originally at par (because technically they are a time deposit) with principal plus interest payable at maturity. Payment of CD's at maturity is made in federal funds,[18] and thus payment is "same day" rather than the "usual way" (meaning next day or up to four days) form of payment of most other instruments.

Repurchase Agreements

In order to finance the billions of dollars of government securities held in inventory, the approximately 19 government securities dealers (of which five are banks) must "borrow" from banks and nonfinancial corpo-

---

[18] *Federal funds* is the term used to denote the market for excess deposits banks have with the Federal Reserve Bank. When a firm finds that its deposits exceed its requirement, it may loan its excess for the going rate on federal funds. Since all member banks must keep deposits with the Federal Reserve, transfer of funds is made via telegraphic notification and a bookkeeping change is made.

While payment of matured CD's is made via federal funds as a matter of course, payment in federal funds also may be possible for the principal money-market instruments. Arrangements of this type are not always possible, however, and one- to four-day payment may result.

rations. In this respect, government securities dealers are rather like finance companies: they make a profit—and thus justify their existence —by borrowing money at one rate and loaning it at a higher rate. But the way in which government securities dealers finance their operation is, for the most part, different from finance companies. Finance companies sell commercial paper. Government securities dealers do not finance most of their operations by issuing paper, but rather by entering into an agreement to sell and later repurchase government securities. Thus there is not a "note of indebtedness" as with commercial paper, but rather only an agreement that the dealer with repurchase the given amount of government securities at a higher price than the sale price. The securities are not pledged; physical transfer of securities actually takes place and is an integral element in this type of financing. The agreement between a dealer and the purchaser is in this case the contract and is called a *repurchase agreement* or RP.

At first sight the use of RP's seems like an awkward and rather indirect way for government securities dealers to finance their activities. It might appear that a "call loan" would be more direct. Since all of the principal dealers are in New York, however, the apparent enigma is resolved by noting that the usual call-loan rate is above the rate on short-term government securities, which constitute 75 to 80 percent of the inventory of the dealers. With a steady demand for call loans by (stock and bond) securities dealers, New York banks felt no particular need to make loans to government securities dealers at rates that would allow the dealer to make a profit. So naturally the dealers turned to other sources of financing. In January 1967 the dealers had a total of just under $5 billion financing (daily average), of which New York City banks supplied only $1.5 billion. Lacking the mammoth stock markets of New York and the demand for call loans thereby created, many banks in other parts of the country found that they could purchase RP's and thus somewhat approximate a call loan. Additionally, about $1 billion of the current financing of the dealers comes from nonfinancial corporations. The relative percentage of financing via these corporations has declined over the years, however, as the CD's were developed and the market for commercial paper and banker's acceptances improved.

There are three basic types of RP's. (i) The overnight transaction is just what the name implies. A purchase is made one day, and the repurchase is effected the next day. (ii) If desired by both parties, the transaction may be renewed on a day-to-day basis. If the dealer and the purchaser wish, an open repurchase transaction may be effected, giving either party the option to terminate the agreement at call, or upon some degree of notice, say five days. (iii) If the purchaser knows the date of his need for cash, he can elect a fixed-date repurchase transaction. In this instance an agreed-upon termination or repurchase date is set at the start.

Owing to the need for physical exchange of securities, most corporations will find the purchase of RP's considerably less desirable than the purchase of Treasury bills (which will probably have a very slight yield advantage to the firm).[19] If the firm is based in the New York area, then this transfer problem would be immaterial; but if the firm is not in New York, it will find it necessary to appoint a trustee for the securities, usually a bank or trust company. If the firm is already a depositor of a New York bank, or its bank has a branch in the city, then the problem is also small, but still a little bit of trouble. This is particularly so since the major banks in the principal cities can effect a purchase or sale of Treasury securities on the strength of a telephone call, and the corporate portfolio manager is spared the problem of transferring possession.

For portfolio managers who have a high aversion to any risk with respect to short-term m_c investments, however, the repurchase agreement may be used. For a relatively low yield he can secure the peace of mind that a known amount of cash will be available on a given date. But is a government security dealer really any safer than a prime bank or finance company? It is true that the Federal Reserve has a great amount of interest in the dealers, but for practical purposes the yield differential between RP's and prime CD's, prime banker's acceptances or prime commercial paper seems hardly worthwhile. It is little wonder that only $1 billion of corporate funds are invested in RP's.

However, the fact that RP's are paid for and sold with the use of federal funds, coupled with the fact that funds can be invested for very short periods of time with near certainty of recouping the principal amount, makes the RP worthy of consideration in specific circumstances.

Federal Agency Securities

Like RP's, federal agency securities are priced by the money market very close to Treasury bills. As such, they may be more adaptable to the m_0 segment of the firm's portfolio then to the m_c segment. Unlike RP's however, the short-term issues of the federal agencies usually have a

---

[19]The effective yield on RP's varies considerably—even from day to day. Free bank reserves, coupled with settlement dates for banks, largely determine the rate. On any given day, the rate may be quite attractive, and thus it is wise to keep these securities in mind.

positive yield differential in the secondary market of from 10 to 40 basis points.

There are only five federal agencies that have outstanding securities that have any significance in the money market, and it should be remembered that these issues are not part of the public debt, are not a legal debt of the United States Treasury, and are not actually guaranteed by the government. But since they are issued by agencies that the government established, even though they may not be owned currently by the government, the public has felt that they are implicitly guaranteed by the government.

The five principal agencies issuing short-term securities are:

Federal Home Loan Bank (FHLB)
Federal Intermediate Credit Banks (FICB)
Federal Land Banks (FLB)
Bank for Cooperatives (BC's)
Federal National Mortgage Association (FNMA or Fannie Mae)

The FHLB's lend funds to member savings and loan associations that are raised in the capital market through notes of 9–12-month maturity, and through bonds of several years' maturity. In July 1969 there were outstanding about $5.5 billion of FHLB securities maturing within a year.

The FICB's, in providing loans to production credit associations and various agricultural credit corporations that assist farmers, make monthly offerings of nine-month debentures, of which there were outstanding about 4.2 billion in July 1969.

The FLB's provide long-term credit to the Federal Land Bank Associations which in turn make long-term loans to farmers. Thus the FLB issues bonds with maturities up to about ten years. In July 1969 there was $5.7 billion of these bonds outstanding.

The thirteen Banks for Cooperatives (BC's), which make loans for seasonal needs of farmer-owned cooperatives, issue six-month "debentures" with usually one or two issues a month. Only about $1.4 billion were outstanding in July 1969, however.

In the job of buying and selling mortgages guaranteed by the Federal Housing Administration (FHA) and the Veteran's Administration (VA), Fannie Mae had a total of about $8.1 billion of short-term discount notes and bonds outstanding in July 1969.

In addition to these five principal agencies, the Tennessee Valley Authority occasionally issues short-term notes, but the amount is usually quite small—only about $50 to $200 million. The newly established Government Mortgage Association (Ginnie Mae) will presumably issue short-term securities but the importance of these will have to be established.

Collectively, the total amount of securities of these agencies was about $24.9 billion in July 1969—almost double the level of January 1967. Furthermore, this amount is about four times the average amount in 1962, and places agency money market securities in the area of CD's (usually) and commercial paper with respect to volume.

SELECTING SECURITIES FOR THE m_c PORTFOLIO

Owing to the nature of the m_c segment of the portfolio, the two criteria of most importance are safety and yield. Because the conversion of cash is expected to take place at a given time (within narrow limits), the quick marketability so important in the m_0 portfolio is not present. While it is true that it is possible to dispose of most securities mentioned as appropriate to the m_c portfolio with ease and dispatch, the adroit portfolio manager will select a portfolio from among the appropriate securities with an eye toward yield. This usually means commercial or finance company paper. Certificates of deposit will usually have a yield advantage over banker's acceptances and short-term issues of government agencies. RP's usually have no yield advantage over Treasury bills but do provide for very short-term investments. If RP's continue for more than a few days, however, the investing firm will suffer an opportunity loss. Also, firms not in or around the New York area will probably find the RP of no advantage over any of the other money-market instruments.

For portfolio managers who wonder why so much attention should be devoted to getting a slightly higher yield from one security vis-à-vis another, the reader is reminded that a 50-basis-point (= $\frac{1}{2}$ of 1 percent) increase in yield for one year means $50,000 (before taxes) on a $10 million portfolio. This should warrant the extra attention needed to find out the current yield differentials on the various money-market instruments. (It might even pay the portfolio manager's salary!)

FREE (m_f) MARKETABLE SECURITIES

In Chapter 2 we defined free marketable securities to be that portion of M not needed for the m_0 component (to service the cash account) or the m_c segment (interest earning, but "earmarked" funds). Thus

$$m_f = M - (m_0 + m_c) \tag{3-2}$$

Unless the firm is in the business of holding and trading marketable securities, and unless some securities are held for the porpose of controlling a nonintegrated subsidiary or for similar purpose, the m_f securities are essentially redundant. But redundant or not, they still represent an asset of the corporation and should be managed with all the acumen of any other asset category. Unfortunately for the stockholders of most firms, this is not usually the case. Owing to a failure to trichotomize the portfolio according to need, the m_f segment is very often kept invested in securities with high safety and marketability at the expense of yield to an extreme extent.

Many firms act as though a loss of principal in any issue is untenable. But why? Nonregulated, nonfinancial corporations have no reason to act as though they were a life insurance company (whose losses of principal must be charged against invested capital) or banks.[20] Instead, the performance of a portfolio must be judged by the overall holding period yield, given the risk coefficient assumed. Furthermore, the reader is again reminded of the work of Markowitz[21] that demonstrated that the variance of a portfolio might be less, with prudent diversification, than the expected variance of the individual components of the portfolio.[22]

It would be most difficult to recommend the composition of the m_f segment of the total portfolio, but several facts may assist the manager.

First, with corporate income taxes (federal and state) in the order of 55 percent, the attractiveness of tax-exempt bonds is apparent. Since state and municipal bonds are not subject to taxation on their interest, a market yield of 3½ to 7 percent is the equivalent to 7 to 15 percent on a taxable bond. If investments are made in nontaxable bonds, however, the investor should check its grade (Moody's or Standard and Poor's) and also ascertain whether it's a general obligation of the respective governmental unit.[23] Usually, general obligations will sell for a slightly lower

---

[20]I suspect many firms act this way because the securities portfolio manager once worked for a bank, life insurance company or other financial institution.

[21]See footnotes 5 and 6 above.

[22]See also a recent proof regarding diversification of a portfolio, Paul A. Samuelson, "General Proof that Diversification Pays." *Journal of Financial and Quantitative Analysis*, March 1967, pp. 1–13.

[23]Many communities had their bonds graded many years ago, and the current rating may not be representative. Choice residential communities that were once sleepy suburbs are an example.

yield than, for example, revenue bonds.[24] With care and attention, it should be possible to fund the entire portion of the m_f portfolio devoted to debt securities with tax-free municipals.

Striving for a relatively high yield in a bond, however, may be quite dangerous. Below a grade of Moody's B or Ba, the market yield rises sharply, but the assumed risk usually rises faster. Furthermore, if appreciation is sought in the bond segment of the portfolio, convertible debentures offer much more promise than a low-grade—even though low-priced—bond. Currently there are well-graded convertibles selling to yield 4¼ to 5½ percent (and a few even more), taxable interest. If appreciation accrues (because of a rise in the stock price) to the convertible, however, the maximum capital gains tax is 25 percent.

Since 85 percent of dividend income to a corporation is tax-exempt,[25] the effective tax rate on dividend income (to a corporation in the usual tax bracket) is about 7½ percent. Thus high-grade preferred stocks may provide an excellent after-tax yield to a corporation. In a rising market, blue-chip stocks may also provide a good after-tax dividend yield, plus appreciation taxable at the capital-gains rate. However most portfolio managers find speculation in common stocks (or other securities) to be anathema to their situation. But firms do not need to carry this to the other extreme of ultraconservatism.[26]

MECHANICS OF MONEY MARKET TRADING

One of the common problems of students and inexperienced portfolio managers regarding money-market instruments is a lack of awareness of how and where to buy these several securities. Unfortunately there is an aura about these securities which suggests that only the most experienced financiers of Wall Street could possibly handle the purchase and sale of CD's, banker's acceptances and such securities, or effect a "repro" (purchase of an RP). Nothing could be farther from the truth. Any transaction that can be effected in the money-market district of New

---

[24]A revenue bond is dependent upon the proceeds of the people using the improvement for payment of principal and interest—for example, a sewer bond or a stadium bond. Whether a bond is a general obligation or a revenue bond is taken into consideration when ratings are made.

[25]With some restrictions, particularly as regards the source of income of the firm paying the dividend.

[26]The author knows of a firm with its entire portfolio of over $100 million invested in Treasury bills! But they were quick to explain that their bank did all of the purchasing and selling and thus relieved the firm of all the "trouble and bother of handling the details."

York City may be effected in any state of the Union.

There are two principal routes a prospective purchaser may take. The first, and certainly the easier of the two, is to utilize the services of the investment department of the firm's (principal) bank. In the main banks in all principal cities there will be a department that is not only versed in money-market instruments, but usually quite willing to effect transactions. If the firm is a reasonably good customer of the bank, this service usually will be performed without charge.[27] But keep in mind the bank's position: if the firm draws funds out of a cash account in order to invest in short-term securities, this is a loss of interest-free money to the bank. Today's active competition between banks is a powerful counter-vailing force, however, and even if the bank's assistance means a lower balance in the firm's account, most banks when put to the test would rather cooperate in the firm's portfolio management than lose the account to a competitor who will assist the firm. Some guidance and an active interest from the firm should enhance the relationship—and probably add some income to the portfolio.

The second technique is something of a "do-it-yourself" approach. Commercial paper may be purchased directly from some large corporate and finance company issuers. Ford Motor Credit Company, General Motors Acceptance Corporation, Household Finance and Beneficial Finance are illustrations of large direct issuers of commercial paper. CD's and banker's acceptances may be obtained directly from issuing banks.

Additionally, there are a number of investment bankers and broker-age firms that either make a market in some forms of money-market instruments, or will arrange for the purchase or sale of such securities. Solomon Brothers and Hutzler, with offices in principal cities, has been active in the commercial paper field, as well as most of the other securities mentioned. The First Boston Corporation, Lehman Brothers, and Goldman Sachs & Company are also examples of investment firms that handle money-market, municipal, and other securities. In fact over 50 investment banking and brokerage firms can arrange (one way or another) for the purchase of any securities desired. Whatever these broker-age firms can do, however, an active investment department of a large bank (or a correspondent bank of a smaller bank) can do as well. The route that is taken will have to be the choice of the firm; the point of this

---

[27]Recently some banks have started placing a fee (in the order of $5 to $20) for each "transaction." In many cases this fee applies if the transaction is for less than, say, $100,000.

matter of control and collection expenses. In the following sections of this chapter each of these topics will be discussed.

HISTORICAL TREATMENT OF ACCOUNTS-RECEIVABLE MANAGEMENT

Throughout the 1930's and 1940's in most schools of business in the United States, accounts-receivable management was taught under the heading "Credits and Collections." Credits and Collection, as a separate course, came under fire from critics of business-school curricula because the courses and the textbooks used therein were almost wholly descriptive of the work of a "credit department" and not as analytical as most other courses in business.[1]

In an effort to respond to these criticisms, overreaction took place and, in large part, the subject of accounts receivable went into eclipse. The usual textbook treatment, consisting of a chapter or less, was couched in the same descriptive framework or was based on the famous "four C's" of credit—capital, character, conditions, and capacity. The specific definitions of each of these terms varied somewhat by writer, but in essence this is what is meant by each:

1. *Capital* refers to some measure of the size of the prospective customer. This could be the absolute size of the equity or net worth of a firm, or it could also allude to the absolute size of the total assets.

2. *Character* refers to the reputation of the prospective (or old) customer and/or to the prominence of an individual in the management of such firms. In this sense, if a firm or an individual was known to be the type that would pay its bills, this was a strong factor in determining not only whether to sell to the firm or not but also the size of the line of credit extended.

3. *Conditions* is quite an ambiguous term and refers to the business conditions not only of the customer (and his industry) but the credit-granting firm (and its industry). *Ceteris paribus*, if the credit-granting firm's business was down he would be inclined to accept weaker credit risks. If the customer's industry's business conditions were down, some concessions might seem in order.

---

[1] *Cf.* Robert A. Gordon and James E. Howell, *Higher Education for Business* (New York: Columbia U.P., 1959) and Frank C. Pierson *et. al.*, *The Education of American Businessmen* (New York: McGraw-Hill, 1959).

4. *Capacity,* probably the most vague of the four terms, in general refers to the debt-paying ability of a customer. Here, quantitative ratios—*e.g.*, the current ratio, the acid test, and the debt-equity ratio—would be marshaled to show a firm's "capacity."

There is undoubtedly a good amount of wisdom and explanatory power embodied in each of these concepts, but, like the liquidity-preference theory discussed in Chapter 2, these terms are not decisive *per se.* Furthermore, discussions couched in terms of the four C's left the matter of credit *terms* quite untouched and, in general, failed to provide a model for individual decision.

A major break with the traditional approach to accounts-receivable management occurred when Beranek treated the subject in Chapter 10 of his *Analysis for Financial Decisions.* [2] Much to Beranek's credit, he was apparently the first to specifically discuss credit terms as variables in the decision process. Also in the early 1960's Haskel Benishay applied several quantitative tools to the question of accounts-receivable control and has since expanded on this prior work. [3] Specific citation to Benishay's other works will be made below and in the list of readings.

While the work of these two authors and a few others, has done much to advance a vigorous theory of accounts-receivable management, the general subject is still in a rudimentary stage. What follows therefore is an extension of the work of these two authors. Indeed, the present writer owes them much for their inspiration, yet feels that a *general theory* of the subject has yet to be produced. Owing to the paucity of data available on a prospective customer it may be that a very rigorous approach is not possible. In any case, it is incumbent upon financial managers to examine the matter in as analytical a way as possible.

CRITERIA FOR SUCCESS OF ACCOUNTS-RECEIVABLE MANAGEMENT

A matter of central importance in any effort to establish an accounts-receivable program is deciding upon criteria for success of such a program. Further, it is necessary to relate a change in any variable in the process to the selected criteria.

Owing principally to the fetish for ratio analysis that has been wide-

[2]Beranek, *Op. cit.*
[3]Haskel Ben Ishay, "Neglected Area of Accounts Receivable Comes Under Study," *Business and Society,* Autumn 1961, pp. 29–34.

spread for many years, an often used criterion has been the *minimization of bad-debt expense.* But as will be shown in more detail below, this is probably the most undesirable criterion for most firms—especially manufacturing firms. It is true that active pursuit of this minimization may reduce investment in accounts receivable, but at the same time this may have negative effects on sales and profits. Instead of a minimization what is needed is an *optimization.*

If, as argued in previous sections, maximization of profit[4] is the goal of the firm, then profit must certainly be a criterion for accounts-receivable management. As a forerunner to profit, however, is the matter of sales. As will be explained in more detail, sales maximization is *per se* not necessarily the appropriate object. Rather an optimum level of sales—to effect the maximization of profit—should be sought.

The question of the volume of receivables is a difficult and a rather ambivalent matter. If we think of profit as rate of return on investment (ROI), then the implication of a minimum accounts-receivable volume (*i.e*, the dollar amount of accounts receivable on the books of the firm) coupled with an increased rate of return on sales (net income) will produce an increase in this measure of profit. But unfortunately there is interdependence in these two goals. As a minimization in the volume of receivables will most likely lead to a reduction in sales with a possibly corresponding decrease in profit (as a rate of return on sales), it is thus apparent that some sort of optimumization of the volume of receivables must be attempted in this case, too.[5]

In summary, therefore, the criteria against which the variables in the problem will be measured are *sales, profit* (and in this context this will mean net income from sales), and the *volume of receivables.*

VARIABLES IN THE CREDIT PROCESS

The variables in the general credit policy of the firm are basically (1) the cash discount, (2) the cash-discount period, (3) the credit period, and (4) the collection expense. The effect of variation in each of these vari-

---

[4]Or possibly some sort of "optimum profit" may be used instead.

[5]By implication, Beranek uses *rate of collection* as a criterion for accounts-receivable policy (in Chapter 10 of *Analysis, op. cit.*) But this is merely a derivative of the volume of receivables, *given the credit terms.* Thus, while we recognize that rate of collection may be of concern in some unusual cases, this matter will not be treated as a separate variable or criterion in this chapter.

ables may be seen in sales, profits, the volume of accounts receivable, and the probability of collection.

The Cash Discount

The cash discount is the percentage reduction in the face amount of an invoice which the customer may deduct if the bill is paid on or before a certain date. For example, credit terms may be expressed as *3/10, net 30.* The 3 in this case would be *3* percent; the *10* refers to the cash-discount period, and the term *net 30* refers to the credit period.

The origin of the cash discount is obscured by time, but it is indeed an old practice. Presumably it is an enticement to get firms to pay promptly, *i.e.*, within the cash-discount period. For the most part, the amount of the cash discount will vary from ½ to 5 percent, with 2 or 3 percent being quite common. The prime determinant of whether the discount is 1, or 2, or 3 percent, or even 5 percent in a few cases, seems to be industry practice. Or more to the point, the practice in many industries appears to be rather like Topsy—it ". . . just growed."

Whether or not a cash discount affects sales (in a positive way) is a function of the size of the discount and the *elasticity of demand*[6] for that particular cash discount (relative to a discount just above or below the one in question.) See Figure 4-1.

---

[6]Price elasticity of demand is a parameter that refers to the responsiveness of the quantity of a product that consumers are willing to take to changes in its price, given the demand curve for the product. If the quantity taken is quite responsive to price changes, a decrease in price may increase the total amount of money spent on the product; this is called "elastic demand." If the quantity taken is not responsive to price changes ("inelastic demand"), a decrease in price may decrease the quantity of money spent on the product (but not unit sales). Price elasticity (E_d) is defined as the relative change in the quantity of a product demanded divided by the relative change in the price:

$$E_d = \frac{\dfrac{Q_1}{\Delta Q}}{\dfrac{P_1}{\Delta P}} = \frac{Q_1 \Delta P}{P_1 \Delta Q}$$

If we assume that the number of sales at price P_1 are Q_1, where $P_1 = P_0 = \triangle P$, now offered, and that if we reduce the price by $\triangle P$ the number of sales would increase by $\triangle Q$; then with reference to the figure below we can compute the price elasticity of demand as

$$E_d = \frac{P_1 \Delta Q}{Q_1 \Delta P} = \left(\frac{5}{10} \right) \left(\frac{10}{1} \right) = 5$$

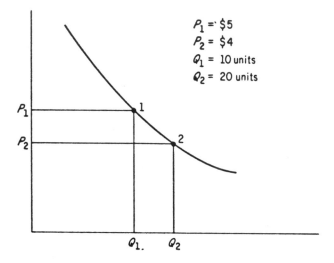

Figure 4-1. Price elasticity of demand.

Since rationally, the cash discount *C.D.* amounts to a *decrease* in price, it would be normal to assume that sales S (in units) would go up as the cash discount was increased from o percent to, at the absurd upper limit, 100 percent (Figure 4-2).

Note that the demand function does not intercept the sales line at the origin o because the explicit assumption made in Figure 4.2 is that

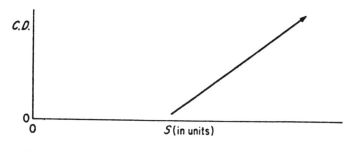

Figure 4-2. "Normal" elasticity of sales (in units) with respect to cash discount.

When the value of E_d is greater than one, the total sales dollars ($P \times Q$) will increase with a decrease in price. When the value of E_d is less than one, the total sales dollars will decrease. There is no change in sales dollars (dollars, not units) if E_d is equal to one. Therefore, in our example both the number of items sold and the dollar volume of sales would increase if the price were reduced.

some sales would be made even if there were no cash discount, *i.e.,* at zero cash discount.

Figure 4-2 also shows sales in *units,* not dollars, because whether total dollar sales increase or not while varying the cash discount is, again, a function of the elasticity of demand. If demand in units were rather *inelastic* with respect to the cash discount (and thus price), total dollar sales could decline as the cash discounts were increased. This is illustrated in Figure 4-3.

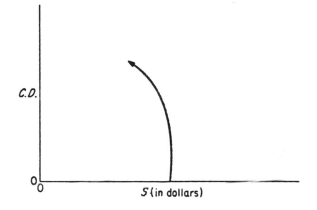

Figure 4-3. Elasticity of dollar sales with respect to cash discount.

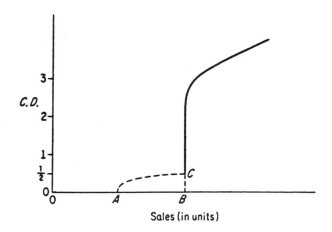

Figure 4-4. Kinked elasticity.

Instead of being elastic or inelastic over the whole range of possible cash-discount rates, a manufacturing firm may find that it faces a kinked function. Thus over the usual range of cash discounts, say, between ½ percent and 3 percent, the function with respect to sales in units may be inelastic, but above this range elasticity may start. Figure 4-4 illustrates this.

The nature of the function below point *C* is moot. If it drops straight down to *B,* then sales would be virtually unaffected from a zero to a 3 percent cash discount.

What determines whether or not the demand function is inelastic over the lower range of cash discounts appears to be a function of the size or importance of the purchase order to the firm's customer. For example, if a firm was negotiating for an extremely large order (relative to the situation), it would expect to have all of its credit terms (plus all other aspects such as price and quality) scrutinized most carefully. In this case the difference between a 1 percent and a 3 percent cash discount might make a great deal of difference in the negotiation.

On the other hand, the author knows of the following situation involving one of his graduate students who began analyzing his firm's cash-discount policy. He divided his sales into three categories: (1) industrial, (2) distributor, and (3) "other" (O.E.M. or original equipment manufacturers, government, and "walk-in" orders). He sold a product that was rather low-priced per unit (paint) and that had a rather standard price per unit. He perceived that most orders from industrial firms were for dollar amounts in the order of $50 to $500, and that it was the practice of most painters to specify a brand of paint in the purchase requisition. Further, he sensed that as long as his price per gallon remained the same and was in line with the competition, few or no questions would be raised over the credit terms. At the time, he was quoting "3/10, net 30," but after the analysis he changed his terms to "net 10," thus eliminating the cash discount. Since he was dealing with established firms (for the most part) the immediate and lasting effect was approximately a 3 percent increase in sales *dollars* to this segment of his total business. (The positive effect on profit, volume of receivables, and the probability of collection is discussed below.)

The cash-discount effect on the volume of receivables is a direct and approximately proportional function of the cash-discount elasticity with respect to sales in dollars. Rate of collection, on the other hand, may not be in direct proportion. If the firm's customers are for the most part discounting their invoices, then whether or not the total dollars received increases is a function of the trade-off between the increase in sales (assuming some elasticity) and the reduced amount of the payment be cause of the cash discount. In general, the relative increase in sales (in dollars) must, *ceteris paribus*, be more than proportional to the *absolute* increase in the cash discount for the rate of collection to increase.

As with the volume of receivables, the effect of a change in cash discount on profit (rate of return on sales) is conditional on the elasticity of demand with respect to the relevant change. If demand is relatively inelastic over the usual range for cash discounts, then a decrease in the cash discount will have a desirable inverse effect on gross profit and probably on net income before taxes. If a firm does think that demand with respect to the cash discount is rather inelastic, then a decrease from 3 percent to 2 or 1 percent may produce an immediate stimulus to a skimpy gross profit. A reduction, or more particularly, an elimination of the cash discount, may produce anomalous results with respect to the ROI, however. If a firm were to eliminate the cash discount and subsequently found that many firms were not paying within the net 10 days allotted, then such a change may, but not necessarily will, adversely affect ROI. It is possible for net income to increase by an amount sufficient to offset the increased volume of receivables due to a lengthening of the average age of the receivables.[7]

The cash discount ostensibly affects the probability of payment in a positive manner inasmuch as it tends to encourage prompt payment. But using the cash discount as a primary means of preventing bad debts is likely to be futile. If a customer is in a serious position of cash insufficiency, he will most likely not be discounting any invoices—irrespective of normal cash discounts offered—and, instead, be exceeding the credit period. An additional point, however, is that a lower cash discount may generate a little more cash and thus provide a better cushion to absorb bad debts.

The Cash Discount and Credit Periods

While the cash-discount period is technically a variable, it is usually treated as a parameter. Ten days is about the minimal period, for practical

---

[7]On this point is is particularly imperative for the reader to relate this discussion to specific circumstances at hand. If the firm's customers consist of particularly large or prominent blue-chip firms, it may be that invoices will be processed routinely. If the firm is dealing with less reputable firms, or undercapitalized firms, a firm with no cash discount may find its volume of receivables soaring with the firm's customers "doing business on your money," to use the vernacular.

purposes, that can be allowed to permit an invoice to be mailed, received, and a check written.

When variations do occur in the cash-discount period, it is usually the result of what is termed "seasonal billing." In this case, shipments are made before the season with the cash-discount date occurring after the season, by a month, or so, before the net due date. Garden supplies and seed, for example, might be shipped in April, with the discount date fixed at, say, October 1 and the credit period expiring November 1. Since seasonal billing virtually amounts to selling on consignment, a firm must be in a position to finance these receivables for the extended period.

Variations in the credit period are, perhaps, more common and are subject to some manipulation. A lengthening of the credit period has an effect on sales demand, profit, probability of collection and, most importantly, on the volume of receivables. *Of all the weapons in the arsenal of the finance manager, the credit period is possibly the bluntest.*

Unless the firm's customers are the type that always discount an invoice, a strong possibility exists that an increase in the credit period will increase sales, as shown in Figure 4-5.

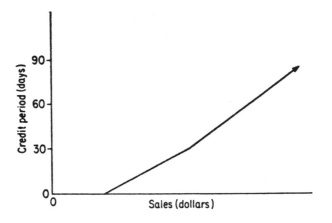

Figure 4-5. Sales demand as a function of the credit period.

If the firm's customers are the type that are apt to be rather undercapitalized there might be a marked elasticity of demand with respect to the credit period. But because of this high elasticity, varying the credit period is quite likely to provoke immediate retaliation from competitors. Several years ago in the Los Angeles area a manufacturer of casual clothing altered its credit period from the industry practice of 60 days to six months. The intended stimulus to sales was immediate. The firm's customers, mostly small retail stores that were quite undercapitalized, canceled orders with the firm's competitors and increased their orders substantially. The principal competitor, however, retaliated just as quickly and announced that they were offering a *one-year* credit period. With a show of strength like this, the firm that started the game, the smaller of the two, reconsidered and immediately changed its credit terms back to the industry standard of 60 days.

The effect that an increase in the credit period has on the volume of receivables is even more pronounced. Because of the demand effect alluded to in the preceding paragraph, a change in the credit period will have a *more than proportional* effect on the volume of receivables. This is depicted in Figure 4-6.

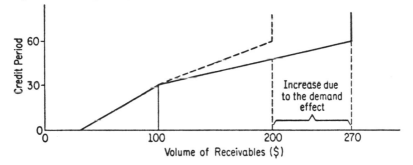

Figure 4-6. Effect on volume of receivables due to change in credit period.

In the example, if the volume of receivables were $100 thousand with a 30-day credit period, a doubling of the credit period to 60 days will *more* than double the volume of receivables. In this case, the illustration shows the volume of receivables increasing from $100 thousand to $270 thousand. But an increase in the volume of receivables from one period to the next is a cash outflow and in this example the firm would have to invest an additional $170 thousand in their accounts receivable within one month. Managers who wish to favor the additional sales and profits that might be garnered by varying the credit period (holding competition constant) should carefully consider the cash-flow implications of such a change.

The credit-period effect on profits is ambivalent. If a longer credit period is offered, assuming competition to remain constant, there will be the aforementioned *demand effect* on sales and thus the absolute net income should rise. However, the rate of return on sales, expressed as a percentage, may not rise. With a more generous credit period, moreover, the firm may feel a degree of price elasticity that might permit an increase in the selling prices. In this case, both the absolute and the relative income on sales might increase, unless offset by a proportionate increase in bad debt expense as will be discussed below.

Since the volume of receivables is expected to increase *more* than in proportion to the increase in the credit period, the effect on ROI will probably be the reverse of the effect on net income to sales. If the firm has redundant cash or marketable securities (m_f), however, then the investment in total current assets may not change, and thus the effect on ROI may still be positive.

In addition to markedly affecting the firm's investment in accounts receivable, a major increase, say, a doubling, of the credit period will also have serious implications with respect to the probability of collection and bad-debt expense. In general, an increase in the credit period will shift the distribution of the probability of collection downward. If nothing else, it will take, say, another 30 days to find out that a customer is in trouble. Also, a lengthening of the credit period may also prompt requests from customers to increase their line of credit, thus compounding the potential trouble. Just lengthening the credit period will probably increase bad-debt expense some, but if this is coupled with higher lines of credit to (all) customers, the effect on bad-debt expense may be most unfortunate and could possibly offset the higher net income due to the demand effect.

The foregoing discussion related to an announced change in the length of the credit period. As mentioned, this is at best a rather blunt competitive tool for most manufacturers. But there is a subtle *de facto* way to accomplish the same effect, at least with some customers. This is the intentional policy of doing business with the so-called slow-pay customers. In most industries there is a group of firms that are thought to be marginal, *i.e.*, they are not as well financed as most and may rely more than usual on the credit offered by vendors.

While any customer that "slow pays," *i.e.*, pays the gross amount of an invoice in 60 or 90 days instead of, say, 30 days, is disdained by most firms, some firms feel that it is quite profitable to sell to a *limited* number of such customers. Generally, these would be customers of fairly long standing and customers who have established a reputation for paying their bills, even if a bit late. The logic behind trading with such firms is for the most part rooted in the selling firm's gross profit. If the gross profit is large enough—and this is quite subjective but, say, at least 25 percent then the selling firm figures that even though the slow-pay tardiness is costing them an opportunity cost, there is still enough gross profit left to warrant trading with the firm. In such cases the firm's slow-pay customer probably would *not* be accorded any preferential treatment with respect to delivery or priority. He would probably remain docile, however, as long as he was behind in his payments to the vendor. This also might provide some welcome flexibility in the shipping schedule for the vendor firm.

THE BASIC QUESTIONS OF ACCOUNTS-RECEIVABLE MANAGEMENT

While analysis and control of the variables in the accounts-receivable policy of the firm are a logical starting point, the basic questions faced by the firm are: *To whom* to sell on trade credit? and *How much* credit to extend? which will usually mean, "How much will the firm permit for a customer's line of credit?" While inextricably mixed, the two questions do not arise always simultaneously. Unless the firm is just starting business, a finance manager would normally face the problem first of establishing (or revising) the line of credit for customers the firm already has, and secondly deciding what to do about a new customer (or one who has rarely bought from the firm in the past). In the latter case, the situation is usually a one-shot matter, *i.e.*, a purchase order is received calling for certain material and/or services for a certain dollar amount. It may be a trial order, possibly as a result of a salesman's efforts, or it might be a blind order from a known or unknown firm. If the order is blind, *i.e.*, comes without any solicitation, the only question is whether or not *to ship that order.* If the order is a trial order, then the vendor firm should start to consider the line of credit for that firm, if the first shipment is satisfactory.

Dichotomizing a firm's customers into "old customer" and "new order" classes also permits a clearer examination of the whole problem, because in the former case the analysis is *not* concerned with any single purchase order, while in the latter case the entire analysis is directed to the one order, including the most important aspect, size of the order.

The Single-Order Problem

In the simplest context, the *single-order* case may be viewed as the following problem. On a probabilistic basis, what is the cost of rejecting the order *versus* the cost of accepting the order?[8]Or, alternately, the question may be expressed as an equation in the form of an inequality which examines the expected gain *versus* the expected loss.

At the margin, in this case meaning one more sales order, the only material cost that is relevant is the direct cost of producing (and shipping) the subject order. In other words, the cost of goods sold, *C.* In a certainty situation, if the order were refused, that which is lost (forgone) would be the gross profit, *G.* Remembering that gross profit may be expressed as sales *S* minus cost of goods sold *C,* or

$$G = S - C \qquad (4\text{-}1)$$

and if we let *P(E)* be the probability of collection of the account receivable, the decision rule would be:

Accept the sales order if

$$G[P(E)] \gtreqless C[1 - P(E)] \qquad (4\text{-}2)$$

To this generalization might be added several refinements. If we take a balance-sheet view of profit, *e.g.,* ROI, then, as Mehta suggests,[9] a factor should be added to the right of the inequality to account for the cost of the investment in the account receivable, (or in other words an interest factor *i* as a function of time *t* applied against the actual investment in the order *C*—or the face amount of the sales order *S'.*

$$G[P(E)] \gtreqless C[1 - P(E)] + i(t)C \qquad (4\text{-}3)$$

Since bad debts give rise to a reduction in the taxable income of the firm, while the realization of the gross profit *G* increases the taxable income, the tax factor may be introduced as a further refinement. In this case, however, an assumption must be made as to whether the firm is beyond the break-even point, *i.e.,* all fixed and semifixed costs have been covered.

---

[8]On this question see Dileep R. Mehta *Management of Accounts Receivables,* unpublished Ph.D. dissertation, Graduate School of Business Administration, Harvard University, 1966), Chapter 3, especially pp. 24–25; reproduced in shorter form as *"The Formulation of Credit Policy Models,"* in *Management Science,* Vol. 15, No. 2 (October 1968), pp. B-30–B-50, and Beranek, *Analysis, op. cit.,* pp. 323–324. These writings have provided much of the inspiration for this section.

[9]Mehta, *op. cit.,* p. 24.

Assuming that all the *marginal* gross profit will be reflected in taxable income, with T the marginal tax rate, the decision rule would be

$$G[P(E)] \, (1 - T) \geqq [1 - P(E)] \, [C - (T \cdot S')] + i(t)C \qquad (4\text{-}4)$$

An "income statement" approach to the decision rule with the tax factor included would be the same as Eq. 4-4 except for the implicit interest factor, $i(t)C$. Thus

$$G[P(E)] \, (1 - T) \geqq [1 - P(E)] \, [C - (T \cdot S')] \qquad (4\text{-}5)$$

Collection Expense and Cost of Investigation

A further refinement of the decision rule shown as Eq. 4-5 is possible by introducing collection expense (B) and the cost of investigation I[10]. Essentially, this process is a type of cost-benefit analysis of further information (investigation). In general, the smaller the dollar amount of the order, the smaller will be the effort (in dollars) put into deciding whether or not to accept the order; the larger the order, the more money that can be spent in investigating the credit worthiness of the (single-order) customer. Similarly, the smaller the order, the less that can be economically invested in collection expense, and vice versa. It makes little sense to spend $20 trying to collect an invoice that has a face amount S' of $20 or less.

Equation 4-5 may thus be restated to include the cost of investigation I, and collection expense B—both tax adjusted.

$$G[P(E)] \, (1 - T) - I(1 - T)$$
$$\geqq C[1 - P(E)] \, [C - (T \cdot S')] + B(1 - T) \qquad (4\text{-}6)$$

The reason for incurring investigation expense I is either to obtain a probability of collection, $P(E)$ or to attempt to *improve* upon the $P(E)$ obtained by initial investigation. In order to illustrate this, consider the following procedure of investigation:[11]

---

[10] *Cf.* Mehta, *op. cit.*, p. 33–34.

[11] The procedure of investigation is couched in terms of information (readily) available and obtainable. Admittedly, the information so obtained suffers from all the vagaries commonly associated with secondary-source information. It is felt, however, that this pragmatic approach is more plausible than an attempt to define a mathematical relationship based on unavailable or insufficient data. Beranek, for example, determines the probability of collection by use of a linear discriminant function of the financial leverage of the firm's customers (*Analysis*, pp. 327–334). I question whether financial leverage (the debt/equity ratio) is really the single most important *measure* of whether a firm will pay its bill to the vendor firm, but in any case, most firms would have much trouble attempting to get the data points necessary to get a reasonably good (linear) fit for such a decision rule function.

1. Check of past records—if new customer or clear record, proceed to step 2. If prospective order is from a customer who was a "bad debt" in the past, reject order unless dollar volume of order is sufficient to warrant step 5.
2. Check *Dun & Bradstreet Reference Book*[12]—(this contains the firm's size code and "complete credit appraisal").
3. Request a Dun & Bradstreet *Report.* (See the accompanying illustrative report Figure 4-7.)
4. Request latest quarterly certified financial statements.
5. Request *Domestic Letter of Credit* from subject firm as a condition of filling the order.

Step 1 should be undertaken for all orders received. The cost of this step might be, say, $2. Step 2 might cost from $2 to as much as $10, or more, for the yearly cost of the Dun & Bradstreet basic service is (1970) $1,150, which includes the *Reference Book* (with six revisions per year) and 100 separate *Reports.* If more than 100 separate *Reports* are used the (current) marginal cost is $4.50 each. Therefore, Step 3 may cost nothing (if all the cost of the basic service is included in Step 2), or $4.50 for all *Reports* beyond 100. To these direct costs should be added the requisite labor cost by the sales department and any associated service (telephone or wire) and clerical (cost of letter) costs.

Steps 1 through 3 would normally be sufficient to accept or reject the order, but if the order is large enough, it may be prudent (or felt necessary) to request recent certified financial statements from the prospective customer.[13]

The fifth step will involve considerable expense to the vendor firm and even more expense to the customer, but it may be used if the size of the order is large enough or the apparent $P(E)$ low enough. The domestic letter of credit is like a foreign letter of credit and merely

[12]Dun & Bradstreet, Inc., is a national credit-reference service of long standing and is, currently, dominant in the field of credit investigation. Virtually every business within the United States is included in their reference service, although no information is available for some firms.

[13]The term "certified" is used advisedly as unaudited statements may be quite in error. The discerning reader will also recognize this as a problem in using Dun & Bradstreet reports, as there is no necessity for a firm to supply this credit agency with certified statements. A modicum of common sense seems called for in this regard as well as the interpretation of Dun & Bradstreet reports. Incidentally, if financial reports *are* requested of a firm it is best to do so via letter and request return via letter. This is so because it is a felony to send material through the mail with the intent to defraud. While a felony conviction for a bad-debt customer is scant recompense for the bad debt, it may help prevent the possibility of fraud because of the possible consequences to the customer.

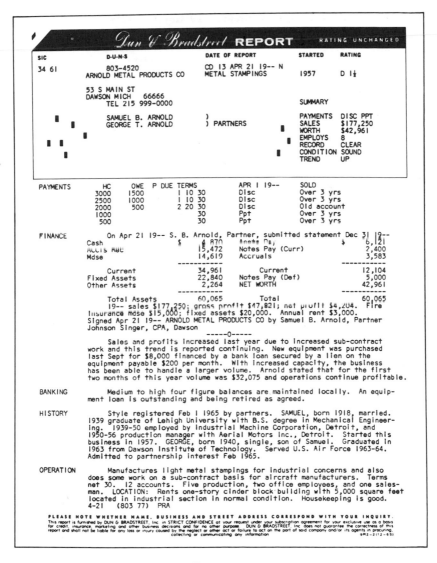

Figure 4-7.

substitutes the credit of a bank for the customer's credit. In effect, a bank guarantees payment of the invoice if the customer is unable to pay. It is through this medium that the probability of collection may be raised essentially to 1 (certainty). The relative size of the order to the customer's

TABLE 4-1 Dun & Bradstreet's Key to Credit Ratings

Estimated Financial Strength								Composite Credit Appraisal			
								High	Good	Fair	Limited
AA	Over	$1,000,000	–	–	–	–	–	A1	1	1½	2
A+	Over	750,000	–	–	–	–	–	A1	1	1½	2
A	$500,000 to	750,000	–	–	–	–	–	A1	1	1½	2
B+	300,000 to	500,000	–	–	–	–	–	1	1½	2	2½
B	200,000 to	300,000	–	–	–	–	–	1	1½	2	2½
C+	125,000 to	200,000	–	–	–	–	–	1	1½	2	2½
C	75,000 to	125,000	–	–	–	–	–	1½	2	2½	3
D+	50,000 to	75,000	–	–	–	–	–	1½	2	2½	3
D	35,000 to	50,000	–	–	–	–	–	1½	2	2½	3
E	20,000 to	35,000	–	–	–	–	–	2	2½	3	3½
F	10,000 to	20,000	–	–	–	–	–	2½	3	3½	4
G	5,000 to	10,000	–	–	–	–	–	3	3½	4	4½
H	3,000 to	5,000	–	–	–	–	–	3	3½	4	4½
J	2,000 to	3,000	–	–	–	–	–	3	3½	4	4½
K	1,000 to	2,000	–	–	–	–	–	3	3½	4	4½
L	Up to	1,000	–	–	–	–	–	3½	4	4½	5

↑ Capital Rating

The Capital Rating is based (in most cases) on Net Worth as shown by the balance sheet, after certain allowances for such things as exempt real estate and intangible items.

Credit Rating ↑

If credit factors such as integrity, experience, financial condition, and payments are unusually strong, rate HIGH. (1st Column.)

If less strong, but all factors add up quite satisfactorily, rate GOOD. (2nd Column.)

If weakness, such as rapid growth on only moderate capital; sluggish receivables or slow-moving inventory; or a deficiency in experience, managerial ability, or character, exists among the credit factors, but there is probability that in time improvement can be made, rate FAIR. (3rd Column.)

If situation described in FAIR has existed for some time, or if the deficiencies are greater than those described in FAIR, and there is little evidence now that the unbalanced condition will be corrected; consider LIMITED (4th Column.)

Source: 10 Keys to Basic Credits and Collections (New York: Dun & Bradstreet, Inc., 1964), p. 36. Used with permission of the publisher.

equity (financial strength) or to the selling firm's ability to *sustain* the loss may be the determinants of the order size to effect step 5.

Determination of Probability of Collection

As with the establishment of the steps of investigation, the determination of values for $P(E)$ will most likely have to be heuristic. If the Dun & Bradstreet system is used, then "composite credit appraisal" ratings may vary, as shown in Table 4-1, from A1 to 5. Unless small retail establishments represent most of the firm's customers, it is unlikely for a manufacturer to have a prospective customer with a rating less than 3½. With subjective consideration to the industry (or industries) of the customer(s), $P(E)$ values may be subjectively assigned to the various Dun & Bradstreet credit appraisals. Evidence would indicate that conservatively low $P(E)$ values should be assigned the "credit appraisal" ratings in recognition of the frailties indigenous to any such ratings. Thus if the gross profit G is large enough, the use of relatively low $P(E)$ values may still permit acceptance of the order. If the use of the relatively low $P(E)$ values points toward rejection of the order, the decision maker, cognizant of the marginal cost of further information, may elect to take the next step in the investigation procedure in order to *improve* the $P(E)$ value. And, of course, if enough dollars are involved, the $P(E)$ could be raised to certainty (essentially) by the use of step 5.

Size of the Order

A further complication is introduced into the decision rule by considering the size of the order (1) relative to the customer's financial strength, and (2) relative to the size of the vendor firm.

In the former case, some (arbitrary) limit must be placed on the dollar value of any single order accepted (as is true with the establishment of a line of credit—discussed below) from a firm with respect to that firm's "financial strength" (or more specifically, available cash flow). A $50,000 order from a firm with $5,000,000 in equity would seem like a small order and appear quite safe, while a $50,000 order to a firm with only $50,000 in equity would be a relatively large order and appear to be quite risky. Dun & Bradstreet suggests that 10 percent of the customer's estimated financial strength be the dollar limit on an order (or line of credit). But there is no rigorous way to support the use of this arbitrary cutoff value.

Beranek attacked this problem by using a minimum acceptable current-ratio value including the addition of the credit the subject firm extends in both the numerator and the denominator.[14]

[14]Beranek, *Analysis, op. cit.,* p. 327.

If A = current assets, L = current liabilities (*excluding* accounts payable), O = trade credit extended by other vendors, and C = credit the subject firm extends, then the current ratio CR may be defined as

$$CR = \frac{A + O + C}{L + O + C} \qquad (4\text{-}7)$$

If A, L, and O were to remain static, then for any CR, C could be determined and would thus be the maximum amount of the order that would be permitted. Unfortuntely, A, L, and O do not remain static and there is no way for a vendor firm to even insist that these dollar amounts remain static. *Even if the current ratio were a really meaningful measure of a firm's ability to pay its bills* (and this is definitely moot), the A, L, and O data observed on a balance sheet are *ex post* data. In short, a vendor firm is involuntarily involved in a gaming strategy. If the subject firm grants x dollars of trade credit, how much will the other vendors grant? Or even worse, how much has been granted by others since the statement was struck? If the situation seems perplexing it is unfortunate, but a fact of life. Happily, the vast majority of business firms are conducted in a forthright and honest manner. But the exercise of a generous amount of business perspicacity, coupled with accounts-receivable controls, is certainly necessary.

The second problem, luckily, is less perplexing, *viz.*, the size of the order relative to the *selling* firm's financial strength or net operating cash flow. In this instance, the vendor firm must be able to answer two questions: (1) Can an order of this size be financed? and (2) What would be the consequences if the buyer failed to pay (and usually this means 25 cents or less on the dollar owed)? The first question involves adequate cash-flow planning, with the "How long?" aspect a stochastic variable. The latter is not really stochastic, for if a bad debt results—a certain fact —the consequences must be met. If a bad debt on an order of the size at hand will cause only lower profits or even a slight loss for the period, management may feel the risk is worth taking. But where judgment turns to folly is the case where the bad debt will bankrupt the vendor firm. This is the business version of Russian roulette—a game not for intelligent businessmen. If the order is so large as to seriously jeopardize the very existence of the selling firm, either a domestic letter of credit, credit insurance, or other safe guarantees seem warranted.

Establishing a Line of Credit

The same "how much" dilemma that befalls a decision maker in the single-order case may be found in the decision establishing a line of credit for a customer. But there is an important difference. The decision to establish a line of credit may be based in part on the immediate prior experience with a customer. This is especially important, for it permits a firsthand appraisal of the customer's attitude toward his bills; moreover, in the words of the old cliché, "actions speak louder than words." Further, the communications that are normally established with regular customers materially assists in providing the "intelligence" that is so useful in appraising a customer's ability to handle a given line of credit.

The line-of-credit problem also differs from the single-order problem in that in the former case usually no decision has to be made with respect to the single-purchase order—all that is necessary is a check to see whether or not the order in question will take the customer's balance over the established line of credit. If not, the order is filled without question. If the order, plus the balance due on the books, will materially exceed the line of credit, a subjective decision must be made.

To think of an "established" line of credit as an inviolable barrier is, of course, highly suspect. Too many factors may affect the business conditions under which the "established" line was set. But here again wisdom must be coupled with business acumen. If a "temporary" situation presses a customer to ask for a higher line of credit, *temporary* measures are called for, not permanent changes. For psychological reasons, it is better to keep the established line of credit, but to permit an extension "this time" than to *increase* the line of credit with the idea of later lowering it.

ANALYSIS AND CONTROL OF ACCOUNTS RECEIVABLE

Once the basic accounts-receivable terms and conditions are set, and a workable, if heuristic, method is settled upon for determining the size of an order or line of credit, the administration of the accounts receivable is assigned to the credit department, or as it is variously known, the collection department. Aside from screening new accounts or regulating the line of credit on established accounts, the job of the collection department breaks down into (1) analysis of the volume and composition of the accounts receivable, and (2) follow-up or agressive collection of the account in trouble or reduction in the volume of receivables when indications point to a general slowing down in payment.

Aggregate Measures of Accounts Receivable

Aside from the obvious and quite important dollar volume of accounts receivable, analysis has traditionally taken the form of a ratio, "average collection period," and an "aging schedule."

In the usual calculation[15] of average collection period, M the average receivables outstanding, is equal to the ratio of R, the accounts-receivable balance, divided by $\bar{S}$, the "average daily sales." The calculation for $\bar{S}$ is: Net sales $\div$ 365. Thus

$$M = \frac{R}{S} \qquad (4\text{-}8)$$

Supposedly, this ratio is a "reflection of the efficiency of the credit department."[16] If it is, then it is a rather cryptic "reflection," ignoring the problem identified in an aging schedule, *viz.*, how quickly *on average* are our customers paying? In order to take this factor into account, what is needed is a *weighted mean collection period, which will be called m'*.[17] In order to construct this weighted mean, however, it is necessary to utilize the total sales figure for the period t_i to t_m, the period over which an account has to be on the books in order to be considered a "bad debt." For firms granting a 30-day credit period, this is normally 120 days (or four months). Let $\bar{S}$ be this amount of sales, and t_i = month "one," t_2 = month "two," etc., with t_m = the month an account becomes a "bad debt." If c = collections and b = bad debts, then

$$\bar{S} = c + b \qquad (4\text{-}9)$$

Let the proportion of credit sales (the accounts receivable) paid during the ith interval after the interval in which they were made P_i. Thus

$$P_i = \frac{\bar{S}P_i}{S} \qquad (4\text{-}10)$$

[15] See Jules I. Bogen (ed.), *Financial Handbook* (New York: Ronald, 1956), pp. 732–733, or any basic text in finance or management accounting.

[16] *Ibid.*

[17] See Haskel Benishay, "Neglected Area of Accounts Receivable Comes Under Study," *Business and Society*, Vol. 2, 1961, pp. 29–34, esp. p. 32; ——————, "Managerial Controls of Accounts Receivable: A Deterministic Approach," *Journal of Accounting Research*, Vol. 3, No. 1 (Spring 1965), pp. 114–132, esp. p. 124; ——————, "A Stochastic Model of Credit Sales Debt," *Journal of the American Statistical Association*, December 1966, pp. 1010–1029. The first article is a statistical model, the second an enlargement of the first, and the third a stochastic model that goes well beyond the early work. Benishay's notation will be used below when possible.

and to get the *weighted mean collection period,* M' can be written as

$$M' = \sum_{t=1}^{n} P'_t$$ (4-11)

with $P'_i = P_i$ if calculated as in Eq. 4-10.

Derived in this manner, the *weighted mean* "average collection period" indicates a measure of *how old* the accounts receivable are, weighted by dollars in months (or other interval). Coupled with information on the rate of change of sales, this statistic can yield valuable information regarding the just-past and, hopefully, the near-future regression function relating accounts receivable with sales.

Examination of the detailed aging schedule will highlight specific problems of a potential or actual nature.

If computerization of the accounting operation is in effect, the possibility of setting variance limits on the mean collection age is not only made possible but convenient. In this case, "normal" variance of M' will be accepted, but abnormal variance (a subjective standard expressed in terms of x standard deviations from M') will trigger more detailed analysis.[18]

Measuring the Effectiveness of the Collection Department

For too many collection managers the name of the game is "minimize bad debt expense." This is either original with the collection manager or comes as dictum from his superior. In either case, *minimization* should *not* be the rational end of a collection department. Instead the objective should be on *optimization* of bad-debt expense. The rationality of this statement is that optimization implies *maximizing profit.*

Assuming for the moment that collection effort is synonymous with collection expense (in dollars) and varies in a *pari passu* manner, then as collection expense is increased, bad-debt expense should decrease, but if carried beyond some optimal point, the money received from reducing bad-debt expense will be more than offset by the money expended on the collection effort. And if this were the only effect, then setting the level of collection expense B would be rather easy. Unfortunately, another effect of increased collection expense may be noted, *viz.,* a *negative-demand effect.*

In Figure 4-8 as collection expense is increased from zero toward B,

---

[18]If this rather sophisticated approach is sought, see Benishay's latter two articles, cited above.

sales may drop *at once* (as from point *Y* to *Z*), or there may be a neutral effect on sales as from *X* to *Z*. But over a range of collection expense beyond some point *Z*, sales will probably decline. This is so because if an inordinate amount of effort is put into collecting receivables (promptly) customers will become annoyed and start shopping else-where, or slow-pay accounts will be squelched, if accepted at all.

Relating the dual effect of a decreasing bad-debt expense to a neutral or slightly decreasing sales demand produces a possible result on profit, as shown in Figure 4-9, from point *X* to *Y*.

Beyond point *Y* the negative-demand effect and the increased collec-tion expense (not offset by a decreased bad-debt expense) both take effect and profits decline. Thus point *Y* indicates the optimal amount of collec-tion expense. Beyond *Y*, bad-debt expense may continue to decrease, but while this might make the naive collection manager feel good, it would be irrational from the point of view of the firm.

The trick in administering a collection department is not only to find the optimal effort, but to reduce the expense incurred in achieving that effort—in other words, to better the *pari passu* relationship assumed above. However, to explore an appropriate strategy for such a collection expense policy would carry this chapter well beyond the intended areas.[19]

Use of Lockboxes

As detailed in the appendix to Chapter 2, another way of reducing the mean collection period of accounts receivable is through the use of the *lockbox*, a post office box rented in a region of high concentration of customers, or at least a high proportion of sales. Customers are instructed to mail their invoices and checks to this lockbox. A local bank is retained to check the box daily, cash the checks, and wire-transfer the proceeds

---

[19]As an example of one firm's attempt to improve results (profitably) from their collection effort, the following was related to me recently. A diversified firm had a subsidi-ary in the Southwest. This subsidiary had small accounts all over the country. Previously, they employed a small staff to write follow-up notices, etc., to slow-pay accounts. Instead of this small group of men (and secretaries), they procured telephone privileges which permitted them to dial for a fixed charge any point in the country. One man was assigned to start making telephone calls at 6 a.m. Pacific time to East Coast accounts, and then on West as the hours of the day went by. Apparently the combination of a personal voice and the long-distance call was just what was needed. The mean collection period declined. Collection expense decline, *and* bad-debt expense declined, with no material negative-demand effect, at least as far as could be perceived.

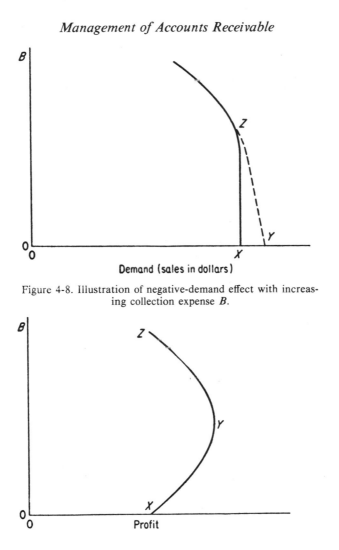

Figure 4-8. Illustration of negative-demand effect with increasing collection expense *B*.

Figure 4-9. Relation between collection expense *B* and profit (rate of return on sales).

to the firm's principal bank. This is followed by mail transfer of the invoice. This procedure reduces the firm's adverse float. The local bank will charge for this service either by requiring a "compensating balance" on deposit or by a specific fee schedule (general and per piece of mail handled), or both.

SUGGESTED READINGS

Ben Ishay, Haskell, "Neglected Area of Accounts Receivable Comes Under Study," *Busines and Society,* Vol. 2 (1961), pp. 29–34.

Benishay, Haskell, "Managerial Controls of Accounts Receivable: A Deterministic Approach," *Journal of Accounting Research,* Vol. 3, No. 1 (Spring 1965), pp. 114–132.

————, "A Stochastic Model of Credit Sales Debt," *Journal of the American Statistical Association,* December 1966, pp. 1010–1029.

Beranek, William, *Analysis for Financial Decisions.* (Homewood, Ill., Richard D. Irwin, 1963), Chapter 10.

Mehta, Dileep R., *Management of Accounts Receivable,* Unpublished Ph.D. dissertation, Graduate School of Business Administration, Harvard University, 1966.

————, "The Formulation of Credit Policy Models," *Management Science,* Vol. 15, No. 2 (October 1968), pp. B-30–B-50.

CHAPTER 5

Management of Inventory

While inventories are scarcely of importance to some firms—for example, service firms—they represent an investment of substantial magnitude for most manufacturing and distributive firms. By classification, inventories may be divided into raw-materials, work-in-process, and finished-goods inventory. The pages that follow present an analysis of the firm's management of its inventories and set forth a simplified model for the control of inventory.

In recent years the subject of inventory management has undergone intensive examination, particularly from operations researchers.[1] Entire courses have been developed to explore the intricacies of various quantitative models and mathematical proofs of the derivation of such models. While recognizing the expansive works on the subject, the treatment accorded inventory management in this work must of necessity be merely a summary. But in keeping with the theme of this book, the approach that follows will be directed toward the *role of the finance manager* in inventory control.

ROLE OF THE FINANCE MANAGER

While the chief executive of a firm has ultimate responsibility for the firm's inventories, and for the firm's investment in such inventories, the functional managers within the firm have considerable influence on the firm's overall inventory policies. The point of importance is that each manager's interest may not be in complete accord with the best interests of the firm *per se*. For example, given the vagaries of day-to-day operation, the production manager would prefer to have no inventory prob-

---

[1]In the bibliography to this chapter there is a listing of some of the newer books on the subject of inventory control.

lems to complicate his functional role. Or more specifically, he would prefer a relatively large raw-material inventory to avoid stockouts and production slowdowns. The old proverb "For want of a nail . . ." is most appropriate to production problems.[2] True, as an officer of the firm, the production manager is cognizant of the "optimum-inventory" concept, but human nature being what it is, he realizes that his job is production management and anything that impedes performing that task is undesirable from his point of view.

By the same reasoning, the marketing and/or sales manager has a vested interest in the finished-goods inventory. Nothing is more frustrating than to make a sale only to find a stockout and an extended back-order delivery date. From the point of view of maximizing sales, the larger the finished-goods inventory the better, as this reduces the possibility of a lost sale via a stockout. And in the regrettable case where the marketing and/or sales manager is judged on the sole basis of sales, one can be sure that he will opt for a large finished-goods inventory.

Purchasing also has an interest in the inventory problem, and if proper criteria are not assessed in evaluating the purchasing manager's role, excess inventories can result. This is so because price breaks (*i.e.*, lower prices) accompany larger orders, not smaller ones. If one wanted to point to how he "earned his way" it would thus be possible to point to reduced costs of acquiring inventory.

Similar arguments could be made for several others within the firm. But it must be obvious to the reader from the above recital that someone must monitor the inventory process to see to it that the *firm's objectives* are met. In short, we are faced with a problem of optimizing the *firm's* goals (usually profit objectives) and not discrete functional *area* goals within the firm. And it is in this way that we depict the role of the finance manager.

It is admitted that in most cases the finance manager will not play the dominant role with inventories that he plays with the other current assets (cash, marketable securities, and accounts receivable), but it should be stressed that in his role as profit manager he must monitor the system to try to achieve the firm's objectives.

---

[2]The author remembers vividly an experience concerning a shortage of lacing tape, in which an assembly line of approximately 400 people was almost brought to a halt. And another experience in which a missing little bag of miniwashers completely stopped a production line of toys. Undoubtedly the reader could add his experiences to the list.

ECONOMIC IMPLICATIONS

The rapid economic expansion of the twentieth century has not been without interruptions, and inventories have played a salient role in these interruptions. In fact, the so-called Kitchin cycle[3] of approximately 40 months' duration, is basically nothing but an inventory cycle. The causes of such a cycle are now quite well known. After the bottom of a cycle has been passed, sales orders increase, and production for inventory is increased. If, as usually happens, production increases at a slightly faster pace than sales, inventories increase. When sales slow at the top of a cycle, the brake is applied to production. With higher than desired inventories, and lower than desired sales, production is more sharply curtailed. Thus we have a recession.[4]

With improved inventory control and faster more efficient sources of internal information within the firm, adjustments to production and inventory can be smoother. So much improved is the process, and the information control, that the sharp slowdown or brake on production is seldom needed. If this process of development continues, it seems reasonable that even better synchronization can be expected. As this happens, hopefully, the Kitchin cycle will be a thing of the past.[5]

OBJECTIVES OF INVENTORY CONTROL

Consistent with the overall theme of this book, the proximate objective of any inventory system should be improved profit of the firm. But of more immediate relevance to the discussion at hand are several other objectives: simplicity, adaptability, effectiveness, and timeliness.

Simplicity

Inventory systems have been developed that range from the utterly simple to the incredibly complicated. But the objective of simplicity does not apply to any one system to the exclusion of the others. Instead, no

---

[3]Most basis works on cycle theory contain a discussion of the Kitchin cycle, and more broadly, the role of inventories in business cycles. One noteworthy reference is R. C. O. Matthews, *The Business Cycle* (Chicago; U. of Chicago Press, 1959), pp. 199–226.

[4]For example, 1949, 1954, 1958, and 1962.

[5]Unexpected spurts or market slowdowns in demand, with the concomitant lag in production, *can* still cause recessions. The reader is cautioned, therefore, not to interpret the foregoing remarks to imply that we *cannot* have a recession. Such reasoning is nonsense. The implication intended is that better control of inventories works materially against the marked recessions of the past.

matter how mathematical or complicated, whether manual or automated, the objective of simplicity can be achieved if the *purpose* and *system* are clear enough to be understood by those having to work with the system or be affected by its operation. This rather prosaic statement is true of any "system," but because this objective is so frequently violated in inventory control it deserves being singled out for special attention.[6] Whatever the system, it must be susceptible of clear and easy understanding *in principal* by all affected parties.

Adaptability

Is the inventory system adaptable to change? Will new products, new divisions, and new needs cause problems with the system? When a system is designed, it may be impossible to consider all eventualities, but the analyst should try to make the system flexible and adaptable to change. Strikes or imminent threats of strikes, governmental restrictions, and most significantly, changes in demand are some of the most important contingencies that come to mind. One word of caution: systems should not be allowed to provide for every contingency possible or imaginable. If this degree of completeness is attempted, it is likely to result in the creation of a monster. Instead, build a system with sufficient checks and balances such that an analyst will be informed of the unusual and allowed to make corrections as needed.[7]

Effectiveness

While a system must "do the job," it is also of paramount importance that management *know* what the inventory system is doing *and* the current status of the inventory. Further, while it is hoped that the formulas (or technique) used will provide proper inventory levels, *effectiveness* also implies a warning system in cases of problems. Depending on the nature of the inventory, stockouts may be intolerable. If so, great care must be taken such that system failure will not cause undue problems.

---

[6]Usually the "incredibly complicated" computer program is so because of a violation of this objective. But as most computer analysts will attest, "complicatedness" usually implies that the designer of the program did not fully understand the problem himself.

[7]This is reminiscent of the *caveat* with respect to administrative procedures: design a simple system to take care of 90 percent of the cases, leaving the remaining 10 percent to be handled by hand. This is "management by exception." When procedures are attempted to handle *all* cases, incredibly complicated systems usually result.

wn in Figure 5–2, during the first period, demand and delivery
exactly as planned. At the time marked by point *A*, the stock
base quantity, a new shipment arrives and the process starts
period 2, demand is heavier than expected (or delivery is
nd it is necessary to draw into the safety stock. In period 3,
s less than expected, but when the *OP* is reached, the "least
ntity *YZ* is ordered. Fortunately when the *YZ* quantity arrives,
just enough to replenish the safety stock, and added to the
not used, *CD*, the total amount on hand is brought up to the
(desired) opening balance level as period 4 begins. If the system
simple, the opening balance for period 3 will not be the original
ntity, but an amount less by the quantity used of the safety stock.
case, Figure 5–2 illustrates the principle of a safety stock.
e amount of units in a safety stock is determined as a function of
ected variance of demand, the expected variance in delivery, the
ed "short cost," *i.e.*, the cost of running out of the material in
on, and as a partial function of this short cost, the cost of investment
safety stock.[12]

Mere installation of a safety stock is no guarantee against a stockout,
ever. If, as noted previously, the safety stocks is penetrated but the
ntity ordered is only *YZ*, problems in subsequent periods are apt to
ear. What is needed is a statistical control device that will note that
en a new period begins, the original target quantity (*YZ* in the illustra-
) will not be on hand, (because of depletion of safety stocks), and that
re must be ordered. Also, this built-in "sensing" system must also be
rt to the possibility that demand is running differently from expected.
demand is more than expected (adjusted for an acceptable statistical
nfidence limit), then the reorder point *OP* must be advanced in time
d/or a larger quantity(> *YZ*) ordered. Even if a computerized system
s used, with this feature built in, it is the advice of many authors inti-
mately familiar with inventory control to have the computer issue a
pecial warning concerning the material in question. In this way expedit-
ing of the purchase order or workorder can ensue with the hope that an
outage will not occur. This is particularly important for class *A* inventory. For class *B* inventory, delays will often be permitted if they occur.

---

[12]Any of the basic textbooks on inventory control mentioned at the end of this chapter contain extensive discussions of the theory and mathematical determination of a safety stock.

If the system is computerized, some weird results may be produced if the system is not designed to be effective in spotting problems.[8] In recent years, however, statistical or programmed checks and
balances have been built into systems, such as payroll and inventory, that
will signal when a highly unusual order is to be processed. Orders for a
certain part may vary from 1 to 1,000 but if an attempt is made to process
a request for more than 1,000, user attention is directed to the apparent
"bug."

Timeliness

Obsolescence is very often a problem in inventory management, and
the term *timeliness* is used to imply protection against obsolescence.
Additionally, the objective of timeliness implies that the system be susceptible of producing reports on the condition of the inventory in sufficient time for management action to be taken.

Obsolescence may be a problem of greater magnitude than management supposes. This is so because obsolescence does not imply bad
material; rather, the material may be quite good, but simply no longer
used or needed. And unneeded material takes up space, which is an item
of cost.

The problem of identifying obsolete material is sometimes a difficult
one. One rather simple solution has been suggested that would list
material in inventory in descending order of usage. Thus, if statistically
it is expected that only one piece of a certain part is used per month, but
there are 12,000 of such parts in stock, the listing would show this part
as being stocked to service 12,000 months' requirements.[9] Obviously, if
computers are used for inventory control, periodic reports showing supply on hand, expressed in time, are relatively easy to produce.

WHAT TO CONTROL

The increasing use of computers in inventory control has made

---

[8]The author was told of a colossal "goof" by a military computer in Atlanta. An order for 120 garbage cans was sent from a Midwest base to the depot in Atlanta. Somehow, the computer misread the request as 12,000 garbage cans. The computer issued shipping orders for the cans in storage, and then proceeded to issue back orders for the balance. Undoubt-edly the arrival of 12,000 garbage cans on the base caused some to question the effectiveness of the inventory system.

[9]This is not as absurd as it may at first appear. The author knows of one case where this was done, and the first page of the report started with an item on hand in sufficient quantity to take care of the next 1500 years! Furthermore, the itemization on the first page went down through 1,000 years' supply.

possible and feasible a degree of *completeness* in control not heretofore available. But because it is *possible* to effect extensive control over *all* inventory does not imply that it is desirable to do so.

Recognizing that some inventory (in some firms) turns over quicker, and therefore represents a larger investment than others, a system has been developed called the *ABC* method of inventory control. *"A"* items are those with the largest investment (as a group), *"B"* the next largest, and *"C"* is that group with the lowest usage (or turnover). One author noted with respect to a particular inventory that 10 percent of the items inventoried represented 85 percent of the annual dollar usage. This would be the *A* group. The *C* group, at the other extreme, was represented by 75 percent of the items, but accounted for only 5 percent of the yearly dollar usage.[10]

To effect an *ABC* system it is necessary to make a study of the total dollar issuance of each part (from the storeroom) and then to rank this itemization in descending order of usage. What would constitute each group is a matter of individual prerogative; all that is necessary is that "breaks" be established. Once this is done, the *A* group would be subject to the most intensive analysis and review. The *B* group would receive fewer reviews (with lower "safety stocks"—explained below), and the *C* group relegated to only minimal, if any, surveillance. Once analyzed, the *A* group might represent, as Niemeyer suggested,[11] items with an annual usage of $1,000 or more, the *B* group might be from $100 to $1,000, and the *C* group less than $100 of usage per year. Of course, these figures are illustrative only.

The types of items represented by the *C* group are, for the most part, those items where only a few are (or were) needed, and a purchase order for the "maximum quantity for the minimum price" had to be issued. For example, if five electrical components (say, diodes) were needed, it may be necessary to order 100 as a minimum quantity.

Of course, this *C* group suggests the prior discussion of obsolescence, and the reference to the fact that obsolete material costs money for storage—if nothing else. Where the distinction will lie is again a matter of personal choice. Most managements would prefer, however, to take the "maximum quantity for the minimum price" and worry later

[10]Robert D. Niemeyer, "Inventory Control," *Management Services,* July–August 1964, pp. 25-31; reproduced in Edward J. Mock, *Financial Decision Making* (Scranton, Pa.: International Textbook Company 1967), pp. 358–370, esp. 368–369.

[11]*Ibid.*

about the disposal problem associated cheaper to store small items for years, in need, than to repurchase a few pieces.

THI

In the hypothetically perfect world, inve be no real problem at all. Least-cost (per unit chased or made and at precise moments (in the would be placed. Figure 5–1 illustrates the proc all variables are known with certainty, the reor that quantity corresponding to the point in time lent to the delivery time for a new shipment (or

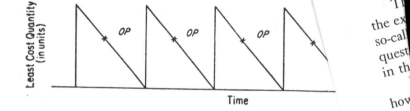

Figure. 5-1. Theoretical depiction of a simple inventory

But what does this oversimplified model assume? F that a deterministic (and realistic) least-cost quantity ca Second, that demand is constant (and, usually, linear) over that the placement of the purchase order or shop worko executed with predetermined precision, and that delivery precise length of time—no more and no less.

Relaxing the second or third assumption gives rise to th "safety stock."

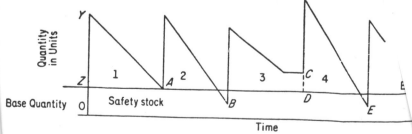

Figure 5-2. Illustration of safety stock.

As sho
time were
reaches th
again. In
delayed)
demand
cost" qua
there is
quantity
original
is overl
YZ qua
In any
the ex
so-cal
quest
in th
how
quar
app
wh
tio
m
al
If
c
a

THE ECONOMIC ORDER QUANTITY

One of the earliest applications of mathematics to a business problem was the determination of how much to order of any one item—the economic order quantity, or EOQ. While there is no general model for the EOQ used by all, or applicable to all situations, even the most complex models are but refinements of the elementary model, and refinements are frequently necessary. Thus, the reader is cautioned to use with discretion any "canned" model, computerized or not, in any specific situation.

The basic EOQ equation given below is really a way of relating the fixed cost of placing an order (a purchase order or a work order if manufactured in-house) and the variable cost of an order. The variable cost, or inventory carrying cost, is expressed as a decimal of the unit cost, and consists of storage costs, insurance, deterioration, obsolescence, and mysterious disappearance; and very importantly, the *opportunity cost* of tying up funds in that inventory (more on this point below). In short, the fixed cost could be minimized by placing one huge order, say, once a year. But this would maximize the variable cost. The variable cost would be minimized by very frequent orders—at the extreme, once a day. Diagramatically, the situation is shown in Figure 5–3.

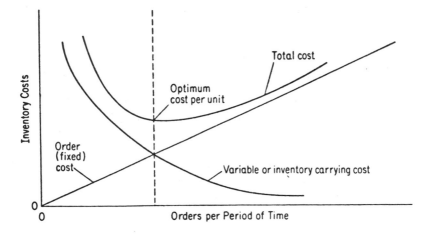

Figure 5-3. Inventory costs versus orders per period of time.

The optimum cost per unit is also the minimum total cost per unit. To derive the EOQ, however, the following familiar equation is used:

$$EOQ = \sqrt{\frac{2OS}{I}}$$ (5-1)

where O = order (fixed) cost per unit
  S = sales per period in dollars
  I = variable or inventory carrying cost expressed as a decimal (percentage) of unit costs.

To express the EOQ in physical units, the formula is modified slightly as follows:

$$EOQ = \sqrt{\frac{2OU}{IC}}$$ (5-2)

where U = usage in units per period of time
  C = unit cost

Note that in the basic formula, demand (*i.e.*, sales or periodic usage) is stated as a given constant. But for many operations, demand is a variable, and not a constant. To correct for this, the use of a probabilistically weighted mean demand figure has been suggested. This requires a probability distribution of expected demand, either based on historical data, or on "educated guesses."

But in an outstanding article, Arthur Snyder[13] reminds us that the EOQ equation stated above merely picks out *one point* on a total cost function. By sensitizing the cost computations, he notes that an EOQ *range* may be elicited whereby the total cost may vary insignificantly over a rather broad range of EOQ quantities, pragmatically speaking. In other words, it is Snyder's contention that total cost curves may be rather flat over an economically significant range of possible EOQ values. If this be true for a given situation, it then becomes possible to vary the EOQ up or down from the precisely calculated EOQ amount.

Taking an EOQ at the upper end of the range would, in effect, take account of demand variations one, two, or three standard deviations

[13] Arthur Snyder, "Principles of Inventory Management," *Financial Executive*, April 1964, pp. 13–21; reprinted in J. Fred Weston and Donald H. Woods, *Basic Financial Management.* (Belmont, Calif.: Wadsworth, 1967), pp. 113–131.

above the expected mean value. As a check on this, all one has to do is to recalculate the EOQ with the larger demand values. This could be done in steps of one, two, or three standard deviations. Thus decision rules could be programmed into the system such as the following: If the EOQ value for the demand figure X plus two (or three) standard deviations above the expected mean demand figure is within the (predetermined) EOQ range, accept the EOQ value corresponding to such value. If the EOQ value so determined by the higher demand figure is outside of the range, accept the top EOQ value of the acceptable EOQ range.

Additionally, management may wish to build into the program additional parameters or constraints. For example, in no case shall the EOQ quantity be a quantity that will not be used in, say, six months, or one year.

Another variation of the model might be to attempt to take account of "short" costs, *i.e.*, the cost of being out of stock. This may be the loss of the gross profit on a sale (in the case of a finished item), or production delays (in the case of raw-material inventory). The latter, incidentally, are usually so large that management would classify any such item as class *A*, and the program would include an overly generous safety stock. In either case, however, the problem would involve an "expected-gain" solution whereby short cost would be balanced against the total cost of order. Since short cost also involves the very real but nebulous factor of customer dissatisfaction, it is a most difficult factor to quantify, however.

ORDER POINT

Having determined "how much" to order or buy, the next question for solving the inventory problem is when to order. "When" in this case means what quantity must the inventory fall to (or below) to signal a reorder of the EOQ amount.

In the simplest terms, the reorder point *OP* may be expressed as

$$OP = \text{lead time} \times \text{daily usage} \qquad (5\text{-}3)$$

If the normal delivery lead time (to make or buy) is longer than the time between orders, it will be necessary to place an order before the prior order is received. To correct for this, Weston and Brigham note that the so-called "Goods in transit" should be subtracted.[14] Thus:

$$OP = \text{lead time} \times \text{daily usage} - \text{goods in transit} \qquad (5\text{-}4)$$

[14] J. Fred Weston and Eugene F. Brigham, *Managerial Finance*, 3d ed. (New York: Holt, 1969), pp. 479–480 and footnote 7.

If a safety stock is used—and this is a "must", at least, for all Class A inventory—the OP must be increased by the amount of the safety stock. Thus, OP would be

$$OP = \text{lead time} \times \text{daily usage} - \text{goods in transit} \\ + \text{safety stock depletion} \quad (5\text{-}5)$$

Snyder[15] uses the more complicated Behr-Manning formula[16] as follows:

$$OP = S(P - L) + F\sqrt{SQ(P - L)} \quad (5\text{-}6)$$

where S = sales or usage

P = production or procurement cycle

L = lead time

F = stockout acceptance factor

Q = units per demand, *i.e.*, units per order

Everything must be in the same unit of time, *e.g.*, months or weeks. Sales or usage is the forecast of future sales or usage based on historical data or "best guesses." Production or procurement cycle is the total time normally required to purchase or manufacture the item. Lead time is the variable that represents delivery time (whether purchased or made). This is shorter than P by the amount of time it takes the firm to generate the

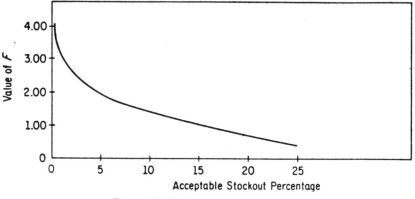

Figure 5-4. Stockout acceptance factor F.

purchase or workorder. F, the stockout factor, is a factor derived from Figure 5–4 and is based on the assumption of a Poisson distribution of demand.

[15]Snyder, *loc. cit.*, pp. 115–117.
[16]Behr-Manning Company, Troy, N.Y.

If the probability distribution of demand for an item is Poisson-distributed it would appear (approximately) skewed as shown in Figure 5-5.

To read the *F* value from Figure 5-4, management must decide what level (percentage) of stockouts it will accept (statistically speaking). The less chance it is willing to take of a stockout, the higher the *F* value, and thus, from Eq. 5-6, the higher the reorder point. If management only wants a 2 percent chance of a stockout, the *F* value would be about 2.00.

Q, the units per demand, is the expected quantity of the item in question that is ordered each time an order is placed. The usual illustration is spark plugs—either six or eight will be drawn by a mechanic at one time.

The Behr-Manning reorder point formula differs from the simpler *OP* (as shown in Eq. 5-5 in that the safety stock is, so to speak, built into the equation. This is because of the use of the *F* factor.

Problems with Reorder Points

A serious problem may develop in using EOQ inventory systems if the program is not designed to take account of situations when the *OP* is surpassed materially by one order. For example, suppose for a particular item the *OP* is 100 units, and the balance on hand is 120 units. If an order (unusually large) is withdrawn for 40 units, the *OP* is broached and the program will place an order for the EOQ quantity. But the same EOQ quantity would be ordered if only 20 units were withdrawn. To account for the fact that the balance is 20 units *below* the *OP*, the program should order the EOQ quantity *plus* 20 additional units. When this is not done, stockouts are more frequent, and yielding to the natural response,

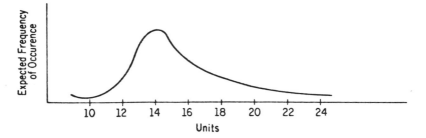

Figure 5-5. Illustration of a Poisson distribution of demand for an item. (Not intended to be precisely to scale).

management raises the *OP*. But this adds to the holding cost of inventory
—a far more expensive remedy.[17]

ESTABLISHING THE INVESTMENT COST

Aside from outage costs, the two basic categories of inventory cost
are the order cost (rather fixed) and the inventory carrying costs. The
basic components of order costs and inventory carrying costs were mentioned earlier, but one component of inventory carrying cost deserves
special attention: the investment cost.

As with investment in redundant cash and accounts receivable, once
again management—and especially the finance manager—is addressed
with the problem of deciding on the cost of investing cash in an asset.

If the firm has to borrow to help finance its inventory, common sense
dictates that the rate should be at least the borrowing rate. But as with
the similar discussion concerning lockboxes, if it is not borrowing, then
the rate should be at least equivalent to the rate it would earn elsewhere
in the firm or, as a last resort, in marketable securities of the *m* type.
But would any of these rates be sufficient? For example, if it were
borrowing money to finance inventory, this implies that other borrow-
ings would have to be at a higher rate as the firm has used some of its
borrowing capacity. If this be so, then some premium ought to be added
to the stated borrowing rate.

Undoubtedly, most managers use as their investment cost their
short-term borrowing rate, possibly with a premium, whether or not they
are borrowing at the time. But another possibility exists. Instead of
looking upon "investment cost" as a cost per se, (whether it be out-of-
pocket as in the case of interest, or opportunity cost in the usual economic sense), it is possible to use a figure that represents what
management *wants* to make on inventory investment—for example, 15,
18, or 20 percent per annum. Such an arbitrary figure would in no way
violate the workings of an EOQ inventory system, but it would affect the
level of inventory. The higher the investment cost used in the equations,
the lower will be the EOQ quantities, and the lower the average inventory level. But would such an approach be sound economics? This author
believes it would be because of the chance to program the course of the

[17]Some newer, highly mathematical techniques sense the amount of penetration
beyond the *OP* and compensate accordingly. Also, the techniques first applied to electronic
servo-mechanisms are being explored such that there is a continual feedback sensing
technique to test the rate of demand as a function of time and expected usage.

firm, and the resulting profit, *provided* management realizes exactly what it is doing. To believe that all one must do to increase profit is to increase the investment cost would be folly. For the finance manager to increase investment cost while the production manager and marketing managers were increasing the safety levels to avoid stockouts would be working at cross-purposes. But if *all* top management works in concert and jointly considers the problem, the investment-cost manipulation may be a very good fine-tuning device for improved efficiency and profitability in the firm. Where the optimum rate is will probably have to be the result of trial and error.[18]

INCLUSION OF QUANTITY DISCOUNTS

In industrial purchasing it is rather common practice to quote a lower price per unit for larger quantities ordered. When this is the case, it is still possible to use EOQ systems, although the computation increases. With computers, however, the drudgery is removed.

The effect of quantity discounts in EOQ systems is to produce a different unit price for each purchase quantity category. For example, the purchasing schedule available on a particular item might be as shown in Table 5–1.

TABLE 5-1

Purchase Category	Purchased Quantity	Discount, Percent	Price per Piece
1	0–10	None	$ 20.00
2	11–50	10	18.00
3	51–100	20	16.00
4	over 100	25	15.00

If the firm had order costs of $5 and investment costs of 25 percent, it would be necessary to calculate separate EOQ's. For yearly sales of 200 the EOQ would be as follows:

[18]Such a situation might be ideal for a simulation model of the whole process; for rather small operations, however, it would be a major task.

Categories	1	2	3	4
EOQ's	20	21	22	23
Purchase quantity ...	0–10	11–50	51–100	over 100

In this illustration, 21 units should be ordered as an EOQ since this is the only EOQ that falls within the purchase-quantity category. The EOQ corresponding to the price for category 1 exceeds the maximum quantity for that category, and the EOQ's for categories 3 and 4 fall short of the needed quantities for those categories.

The reader is reminded that whenever purchase quantity discounts exist, there is all the more reason to use EOQ *range* analyses rather than single-point estimates. Because of the parameters specified in the foregoing example (intended to illustrate only the matter at hand), EOQ range estimates would not have mattered. But in practical situations, particularly where the system is computerized, EOQ range estimates should be calculated with reference to the various price categories in addition to demand.

SUMMARY

The basic inventory problem, after many years of investigation, is still what to control, how much to order, and when to order. With the advent of computers in many business establishments, or the access to a computer through a service bureau, the old question of what to control has been simplified. Even if an *ABC* system, as originally conceived or modified, is used, it is now possible to keep a perpetual inventory of even enormous stocks. While it is possible to have machine errors or "bugs" in the program from time to time, the accuracy of a computerized perpetual inventory has increased manyfold. Lest anyone think that such a system is "perfect," however, one should be quickly reminded that the care and attention of the people working with the inventory, *e.g.*, in counting and issuing stock, is still critical to the total accuracy of the system.

But the more pressing problems of how much and when to reorder are still the focus of any inventory system. Since the big variable in the "how much" question is demand for the item (especially for class *A* and *B* stocks), EOQ equations have been developed to assist the manager. To cope with expected variance in demand (primarily), various statistical techniques have been developed to help determine the size of a safety stock. Other techniques, such as the Behr-Manning system, attempt to build in a safety stock when setting the reorder point. And in recent years operations-research techniques to simulate activity in the item have been developed in order to give tighter control of the system.

Inextricably mixed with the "how much" question is the "when" question, or in other words, the theory of the reorder point. As with the EOQ theory and the safety stock theory, the systems in *use* are elementary at best and should be so considered. The techniques on the drawing boards, plus the increased use of computers to execute the involved mathematics, should greatly improve inventory management in the next ten years.

But in every inventory model there is an expression for the so-called "investment cost" of holding inventory. It is with this very powerful tool that the finance manager works. By changing the interest-rate factor— and the chapter strongly urged a kind of programmed rate—the finance manager can raise or lower the absolute levels of inventory. Further, if EOQ range estimates are used as urged, the *length* of the range, in addition to its relative quantities, can be varied by the finance manager. It is to the role of the finance manager, therefore, that this chapter was primarily directed.

Computer Programs

Virtually every manufacturer of commercial computer equipment offers their users "canned" computer programs for inventory control. Additionally, many such companies will "tailor" their programs to a user's specific situation—either free of charge or for a fee based on the work involved. Computer "software" houses have been started in recent years that have the ability to design and develop a whole system for a firm. Aside from these two sources, private, university, and government sources of programmed systems have appeared in recent years. One of the most comprehensive systems was developed at the Inventory Systems Laboratory supported by the U.S. Office of Education at the Johns Hopkins University. Under the direction of Prof. Eliezer Naddor, the following programs were developed:

ISL-1: Balancing Carrying, Storage and Replenishing Costs
ISL-2: A Determinstic Reorder-Point—Lot-Size System
ISL-3: A Probabilistic Reorder-Point—Lot-Size System
ISL-4: A General Inventory Systems Simulation

The programs are written in FORTRAN and BASIC.[19]

[19]Detailed manuals are available from the Director of ERIC, Room 3013, Federal Office Building No. 6., 400 Maryland Avenue S.W., Washington, D.C. 20202. BASIC tapes and/or FORTRAN cards of the four programs may be obtained (for a fee) by writing to the Homewood Computing Center, Milton S. Eisenhower Library, The Johns Hopkins University, Baltimore, Md. 21218.

SELECTED BIBLIOGRAPHY OF INVENTORY
MANAGEMENT

Since a comprehensive bibliography of books and articles dealing with inventory control would be well beyond the scope of this book, the following is intended as a brief list of some of the newer and/or more important sources.

Arrow, K. J., S. Karlin, and H. Scarf, (eds.) *Studies in Applied Probability and Management Science* (Stanford: Standford U. P., 1962), chapters 5, 10, 13 and 15.

Barrett, D. A. *Automatic Inventory Control Techniques* (London: Business Books Ltd., 1969).

Brown, Robert G. *Decision Rules for Inventory Management* (New York: Holt, 1967).

———, *Statistical Forecasting for Inventory Control* (New York: McGraw-Hill, 1959).

Buchan, Joseph, and Ernest Koenigsberg, *Scientific Inventory Management* (Englewood Cliffs, N.J.: Prentice-Hall, 1962).

Churchman, Charles W., Russell L. Ackoff and E. Leonard Arnoff, *Introduction to Operations Research.* (New York: Wiley, 1957), Chapters 8–10.

Enrick, Norbert Lloyd, *Inventory Management: Installation, Operation and Control* (San Francisco: Chandler, 1968).

Prichard, James W. *Modern Inventory Management* (New York: Wiley, 1965).

Starr, Martin K., *Inventory Control: Theory and Practice* (Englewood Cliffs, N.J.: Prentice-Hall, 1962).

Stockton, Robert S., *Basic Inventory Systems* (Boston: Allyn & Bacon, 1965).

CHAPTER 6

Financing Working Capital

Although the preceding chapters were directed toward the management of working capital assets, the problem remains for the manager, on occasion, to finance these current assets via short-term credit, and sometimes by intermediate credit. Fortunately a portion of the current assets will be financed spontaneously through payables incurred through the normal course of business. When this spontaneous credit is insufficient, however, as during seasonal peaks of activity, the manager must resort to raising specific financing.

If a firm's financial condition is thought to be in a most healthy condition by its banker, borrowing via unsecured notes is a possibility. In this case, the responsible corporate officer, president, or financial vice-president merely signs the note for the firm. The lender (the bank) thus becomes a *general creditor* of the firm. In the vernacular, this is said to be *unsecured* lending, but literally speaking, a signature loan is really the pledging of *all* assets of the firm not otherwise pledged or encumbered. The term of a signature loan may be on demand or for a specific period of time, usually 90 days or multiples thereof. In the former case, the bank is in effect saying to the firm "Pay back the loan when you can, or when you no longer need it." When repaid, interest is usually paid to the date of repayment. In the latter case, the note is due and payable on a certain date and if needed beyond such date, specific arrangements must be made for an extension of time. The cost of a signature loan is usually the same or lower than the secured financing discussed below. This is so because if the bank feels their risk is such as to insist upon a higher rate of interest, they most probably will insist on specific collateral for the loan.[1]

Whether a loan is made on a signature basis or with specific collateral

---

[1] A variant of the signature loan by means of a comaker (or guarantor) will be discussed below.

such as inventory or accounts receivable, the lender—either a bank or finance company—may establish a lending limit on the borrower. In the usual parlance of finance this is referred to as a credit limit and may be effected before the fact, or on an existing loan arrangement. In the former case it might be a formal or informal maximum amount the firm *might* borrow if it so wishes. Or, the credit limit might be the specific amount the lender will loan under an already existing loan arrangement with collateral as security. This credit limit is quite similar to "line of credit" discussed in Chapter 4.

ACCOUNTS-RECEIVABLE FINANCING

Accounts-receivable financing normally takes one of two forms: *pledging* or *factoring*. While the exact form of the agreement effecting the loan (or "financing") by means of the use of accounts receivable varies markedly, the description of the procedures and instruments that follow generalize the processes.

Pledging is the use of accounts receivable as collateral for a loan from a bank or finance company. Since the passage of the Uniform Commercial Code by the leading states, the instruments used to effect the lender's secured position with respect to the collateral have been materially simplified, *viz.*, the *Security Agreement* and the *Financing Statement*. The former represents the contract between the lender and the borrower, and the latter is the form used to file the lender's claim against the collateral with the Secretary of State of the state in question. There is also attached to the Security Agreement a form which identifies the specific accounts receivable offered as collateral. Some lenders insist that this list be updated continuously (say, at daily or weekly intervals) while other lenders are less strict on this point. Fortunately for the lender, the former need to be most fastidious regarding the exact accounts no longer exists where the Security Agreement and Financing Statements (under the U.C.C.) are in use.

Before the widespread use of these two instruments it was necessary in most states to use a "Trust Receipt" arrangement. This was a form filed with the Secretary of State which specifically identified collateral —even accounts receivable. In the case of bankruptcy, any confusion regarding a specific account might subject the lender to "general creditor" rather than "secured creditor" status. It is little wonder the banks and finance companies championed the introduction of the Uniform Commercial Code and the Security Agreement and Financing Statement. And in contradiction to many laws passed regarding debtors and creditors, the adoption of these forms was good for business firms too. This is so because now that lenders have an instrument, and a rather simple one at that, in which they can perfect a secured claim to collateral, they may be more willing to make a loan that they formerly may have denied. In the past, even when a bank made a loan via the Trust Receipt they often considered the loan, in their mind, as an unsecured loan. In many cases this limited the amount of the loan—a matter of material importance to the business firm.

The amount of the loan relative to the face amount of the accounts receivable pledged is a variable depending upon (i) the credit standing of the firm's customers, (ii) the quantity and dollar amount of the respective accounts receivable (fewer accounts are usually considered "better" than many accounts of small value because of the nuisance and expense of collection if the collateral has to be seized), and (iii) the credit standing of the borrowing firm. If the borrowing firm is an "average" to "good" credit risk, and if the firm's customers are large well-established firms, approximately 75 to 90 percent of the face amount of the accounts receivable may be borrowed. For lower-quality customers, 65 to 80 percent of the face amount may be borrowed. If the account (or accounts) receivable is a department of the United States Government, 95 percent of the account—and sometimes 100 percent—may be borrowed.[2] If the account is a subcontract to a prime government contractor it is usually necessary for the bank to require certain affidavits from the prime contractor regarding the nature of his account with the government. Most large prime government contractors are quite used to filing such affidavits on behalf of their vendors, however. In order to have a valid security interest in a receivable from a federal government agency, the lender must also notify the government contracting officer and the finance officer for the contract in question.

A variation of the pledging arrangement described above is an arrangement that might be called "pledging with notification." Under this arrangement the borrower (the vendor of the material that gives rise to the account receivable) notifies the vendee (his customer) to remit payment of the invoice to the bank (or other lender). When the bank receives payment, it deposits the funds in a *Cash Collateral Account* for the borrower. It then notifies the borrower of receipt of the payment. When the

---

[2]The variable here is the rejection possibility, and sometimes the possibility of contract cancellation.

borrower receives this notice, it issues a release to the bank and the funds (less the amount borrowed) are transferred to the firm's regular checking account.[3] It is important to note that under this arrangement, the bank (lender) does not have title to the account receivable, as is the usual case in factoring.

Factoring Accounts Receivable

The earliest used technique for borrowing, using accounts receivable as a borrowing base, is *factoring*—the process of selling at a discount the account receivable to a finance company or so-called "old-line factor." As with *pledging*, there are about as many variations of the technique as there are factors, so that the description that follows must be most general.

Under a factoring arrangement the vendor (the borrowing firm in the prior discussion) transfers his collection and usually his credit screening process to a factor. He does this by selling his receivable to the factor for the factor to collect. The vendor thus receives most of the proceeds of the invoice as soon as the goods are shipped to the vendee. The term *most* is used advisedly as there will be a *discount* to the face of the account receivable representing a charge (fee) and, usually, a hold-back amount until the account is actually collected. The fee may be dichotomized into an interest charge, usually expressed in a per diem way, and a basic collection charge. In the former case the *annual* equivalent interest charge may be 15 to 28 percent. In the latter case, 6 to 10 percent of the average monthly balance annualized would be rather typical. The hold-back amount is a function of the expected returns and allowances to the vendor.

Factoring may be *with* recourse to the vendor, or *without* recourse. With recourse means that if an account proves uncollectable (usually a time limit is set, *e.g.*, 90 days, as *de facto* evidence of uncollectability) then the account is returned to the vendor for legal action or write-off. If the agreement is *without recourse*, the factor will absorb the loss on an uncollectable account. Factoring without recourse involves a higher interest rate—usually an additional 6 to 12 percent per annum—than if the vendor absorbs the loss. From the vendor's point of view, this is practically

---

[3]This gives the bank interest-free use of the funds for at least one day, and sometimes for two or three days, depending on how often transfer notifications are made. On this point many firms under this arrangement borrow by notifying the bank of new receivables and transfer funds of collected accounts at the same time—usually two or three times a week.

always an increase in interest *more than commensurate with* the usual bad debt expense. When interest is expressed as a *per diem* rate, however, it may *seem* to be rather small. To some naive managers it may even seem like a bargain—which it seldom is.

With the so-called old-line factors, factoring is almost always *with* notification to the vendee. This means that the vendee's invoice plainly states that payment is to be made to the factor and not to the vendor. With the increase in the use of factoring, particularly since the early 1950's, *non-notification* factoring has become more prevalent. In this case, payment is sent to the vendor or to a post office box. In the former case the vendor is expected to remit the proceeds of the invoice promptly; in the latter case, the factor may remove the receipts from the post office box directly.[4]

Compared to pledging, factoring accounts receivable is an expensive method of financing. Advocates of factoring argue that this is only apparent and not real.[5] Factoring, they claim, by getting money sooner and by eliminating the trouble and expense of maintaining an accounts-receivable and collection department, is no more expensive than pledging.

The "getting your money sooner" argument is often without moment, however. With most banks today, same-day deposits in a firm's general checking account under a pledging arrangement is often possible. True, this is usually a slightly smaller percentage of the face amount of the invoice than with factoring, but for the difference in interest charged, overall, the price that a firm may pay for the immediacy of the extra 5–15 percent of the face amount of the invoice is substantial. As for the argument that a firm does not have to collect the accounts and thus can "save" this expense via factoring, this too is specious. A charge is made by the factor for this service—it is not free. It may be slightly less or more than a firm would incur itself, but it is not a "cost-no cost" proposition.

A firm denied pledging from a bank would normally turn to pledging with a finance company. When this route is also denied them for one of many reasons—usually financial instability—factoring is available.

---

[4] Recently firms have been established to factor accounts receivable for professionals such as physicians and dentists. In these cases, post office boxes are usually used and any pressure, short of a lawsuit, is exerted through secretaries or nurses in the physician's or dentist's office.

[5] *Cf.* Gerrit J. Popma, "A Behind-the-Scenes Look at Factoring," *Credit and Financial Management* Vol. 65 (May 1963) pp. 31–33, 37, 42.

The higher interest charge may not be the only drawback with factoring. In some industries, *e.g.*, the textile industry, where factoring has been used extensively for decades (why?), a vendee is accustomed to remitting payment to a factor. But in many other industries, factoring is objected to by many vendees. In fact, factoring may cause a type of *negative demand* effect. Because of fear of being "dunned" by a professional type collector, many firms will shift their purchase orders away from firms that are factoring—at least, with notification—and to firms that will collect their own receivables. This may be an ungrounded fear, or one based on "one bad case," but to a vendor firm the justification of the reason is superfluous if the firm starts to lose orders. Thus the higher interest and service charge may not be the only "cost" of factoring.

FINANCING INVENTORY

The basic ways to use inventory as collateral for financing are pledging and warehousing.

Pledging Inventory

The Security Agreement and the Financing Statement, as discussed above in connection with accounts-receivable financing, are also used for inventory financing. In fact, most banks (and states under the Uniform Commercial Code) use the same form for both accounts receivable and inventory.

But, as with accounts receivable, the importance of the new legal documents for perfecting a valid claim on inventory is hard to overestimate. Prior to the widespread use of the Security Agreement and Financing Statement, a *Trust Receipt arrangement* was extensively used. Unfortunately, under this technique it was quite important to meticulously identify and keep segregated all inventory covered by each trust receipt. If inventory was mixed, it was believed that the creditor would be placed in the position of a *general* creditor.

Another technique, that of the *blanket lien*—which attempted to place all inventory of a given type, *e.g.*, raw materials, as collateral for a loan—has also been superseded by the Security Agreement. Therefore, whether a lender used a *trust receipt* or a *blanket lien* arrangement it was felt by many lenders that inventory loans under either arrangement amounted to scarcely more than an unsecured loan. With the advent of the Security Agreement and Financing Statement, lenders have much greater confidence in their ability to enforce their secured position with the resulting implication that they are now, more than ever, willing to loan—or loan a higher percentage—against inventory.

Warehousing

For a very long time warehousing has been a mainstay in the financing of industries and especially in international trade. Under this arrangement, goods are deposited in a bonded public warehouse. The receipts are then deposited with a bank (or other lending institution) and as such are collateral for a loan. To recapture use of the inventory, the loan is repaid—or a portion thereof—and the warehouse receipts are returned to the firm, which in turn presents them to the warehouseman for the goods in question.

Variations of this arrangement are commonplace. They include assistance by the bonded warehouse whereby the warehouse will accept a check in payment for a loan, whereupon the warehouseman forwards this check to the lender at the same time he turns over the merchandise to the borrowing firm. In another variation, the lender instructs the warehouse to release a certain amount of the merchandise periodically to the borrowing firm under a prearranged loan agreement.

A more basic variation is called *field warehousing*. Under this technique, arrangements are made with a bonded public warehouse to bond an employee (usually) of the borrowing firm, and to physically warehouse the merchandise on the borrower's premises. This arrangement is usually used when the material is quite bulky or valuable, or when the borrower's plant is located some distance from the nearest public warehouse. Examples of such bulky material are structural steel or large rolls of paper. Other materials so warehoused might be precious metals and diamonds, film, or bulk chemicals.

In a field warehouse arrangement it is necessary to segregate a portion of the borrower's property and identify it as a field warehouse of a public warehouse. Light fences within the main confines of the plant are used for this purpose. Also, safes and locked cabinets are used for the smaller bulk-to-value material. When the borrower wants certain material, he repays the lender, secures the receipt and, by turning over the receipt to the bonded employee, secures the material.

In this latter arrangement, *viz.*, field warehousing, the actual costs of physically warehousing the materials in a public warehouse are saved, but a fee is paid to the public warehouse for the arrangement and, of course, the costs of getting an employee bonded.[6] Also the employee's time spent administering the arrangement is a cost to the borrower.

Public warehousing in international trade has been widely used for decades, at least, and currently functions quite smoothly expecially in such international trade center as New York, Boston, New Orleans, and San Francisco. Because of the long-standing use of this technique relatively high percentages of value are loaned against such commodities in international trade, *e.g.*, 85 to 100 percent.

What Makes Good Collateral

Aside from standard commodities in international trade—non-ferrous metal ingots, grains and coffee, and standard electrical components—bank lending against inventory is more a function of the borrower's credit standing and reputation than the collateral *per se*. Nevertheless, the nature of the inventory does play a role in the percentage a lender is willing to loan. Raw materials of a generic, standard type or similar finished goods are most acceptable. If "work in process" is also offered as collateral, the percentage loaned will be noticeably smaller—that is, if a loan is granted at all. If raw materials are a specialty item made up solely for the borrowing firm, naturally a lower percentage, *ceteris paribus*, will be loaned. In this latter case, many lenders consider the loan basically unsecured but take a Security Agreement on such collateral as extra protection.[7]

SPONTANEOUS SOURCES OF SHORT-TERM CREDIT

While the preceding discussion concerning the financing of accounts receivables and inventory—or, more strictly speaking, the use of these assets as collateral for short-term borrowing—is available to almost all firms, the more obvious sources of short-term credit are those that

---

[6]Whether the marginal costs to the borrowing firm of storing material on its own premises is zero or some positive amount must be determined in each case. If a firm is pressed for storage space, or must rent additional storage space, then field warehousing may not save as much as might be suspected. In any case, at least the cost of transportation is reduced.

[7]In banking terms, this would be a "secondary" means of payment. In granting loans, banks customarily think in terms of "primary," "secondary," and sometimes "tertiary" means of repayment. With relatively risk-free loans, only a primary means, *e.g.*, the firm's cash flow, is required. On the riskier loans, banks will attempt to setup a backstop in the form of secondary and tertiary means of repayment. In some cases the tertiary means is a personal guarantee by the firm's principal.

arise spontaneously, *viz.*, trade credit, accrued payroll, and accrued taxes.

Trade Credit

A discussion of the normal trade credit accruing to a firm is in effect, the analogue to the previous discussion (Chapter 4) of accounts receivable. In this case, however, the firm is faced with the problem of choosing between firms with varying credit policies. Or, the choice may be between firms with the same formal credit policy, but with different enforcement standards. Other things being equal, the choice of a vendor who permits accounts to slow-pay would be preferred to one who holds the line. But slow pay is a rather ambivalent term and requires some explanation. Some firms, for example, rather indiscriminately permit their customers to exceed their cash discount period and yet still take the cash discount. In other cases, if a discount is missed, they may not put pressure on a customer to pay until 30 days past the end of the credit period.

From the point of view of cost, as mentioned earlier, the passing of a 3 percent cash discount under terms 3/10 net 30 amounts of a per annum interest charge of 54 percent! For a 2 percent discount, the equivalent charge is 36 percent. If, however, the vendor firm delays payment until the 50th day, the effective interest charge is cut in half. But even half of 54 percent is an expensive interest cost, and the smart manager will do all he can to secure other less expensive short-term financing.

Accrued Payroll

The short-term financing resulting from accrued payroll was alluded to in chapter 2. The principle involved here is that the employees give their employer an interest-free loan for the pay period. Thus if employees are paid every two weeks, this is equivalent to an interest-free average loan for one week. Repeated twenty-six times a year and multiplied by one-half the total salaries payroll would be approximately the *total* interest-free loan.

For firms with an unusually short production-marketing period, this source of short-term credit may go far in meeting the total short-term financing needs of the firm. This is particularly true if a firm can get by with paying monthly. It is conceded, however, that this is usually possible only with professionals and/or the management staff.

Accrued Taxes

As with other accrued payables, accrued taxes provide a spontaneous source of credit. Since the federal income tax is the principal tax, most attention must be directed toward it. Prior to 1964 (under the terms of the Mills Bill of 1954), firms were able to pay the first $100,000 tax liability in two equal payments in the first and second quarters following the firm's fiscal year. For the tax liability above $100,000 they were granted, on the average, six months interest-free credit. If a firm's fiscal year coincided with the calendar year, it had to pay its tax in excess of $100,000 on September 15, January 15 of the following year, and on March 15 and June 15. With the passage of the Internal Revenue Act of 1964, the federal government attempted to put firms on an essentially pay-as-you-go plan. After a period of adjustment, firms now must estimate their yearly tax liability and make progress-type payments by the fifteenth of the month following a quarter.

The effect of the "pay-as-you-go" tax provision, of course, is to reduce the "credit" formally involved in tax payments.[8]

For firms involved in retail trade where there is a collection of sales-tax money, this involves a spontaneous source of credit as these funds may be used, interest-free, until the payment date. Employee Social Security (FICA) payments and other tax deductions from employees provide limited interest-free spontaneous sources of credit as these must be paid within three business days of the payroll date. State corporate income and other taxes are also considered spontaneous credit.

OTHER SHORT-TERM CREDIT ARRANGEMENTS

While undoubtedly many variations of the aforementioned sources of short-term credit exist, two other arrangements are popular enough to be cited.

Advances from customers, and occasionally suppliers, may prove a timely source of financing. In this situation the approach is usually made directly to the customer or supplier of the firm. The author knows of several situations, however, where the customer or supplier, sensing a lack of working capital on the part of the firm in question, offered the advance without being asked. Or, in an effort to get a firm to use a certain

---

[8]From a cash flow point of view, a decrease in accrued tax liability is the same as a cash outflow. As firms have had to adjust to the new system, this has reduced their net operating cash flow. Undoubtedly, this contributed to the "credit crunch" of 1966 and 1968–70.

product, a supplier may offer to place inventory with the firm on a consignment-type basis, *i.e.*, the supplier gets paid after the firm sells the completed product and collects the receivable.

In other cases, formal arrangements, sometimes with the cooperation of the firm's bank, are made with vendors or customers for either direct loans (short or intermediate term), or guarantees of loans. The situation prompting either a vendor or a customer to enter into such an arrangement would have to be one in which failure to receive financing from any source will adversely affect the vendor or customer. For example, if a firm is an important customer (say, distributor) for the vendor, and his (the vendor's) business will be affected adversely, there might be adequate incentive to secure the financing from such vendor.

In times of war or national emergency, agencies of the federal government have been quite helpful in arranging, directly or indirectly, credit for suppliers of strategic material. Also, while little used today, provision still exists for V-loan arrangements whereby the federal government (on request or through action of the Defense Department) will guarantee, for a fee, most of the loan made by banks.[9]

Another general arrangement for effecting short-term (or longer) credit for a firm is through the use of a subsidiary corporation. How the subsidiary obtains the funds is varied, but for some large, well-known firms, commercial paper is sold. The reasons for the establishment of a separate firm are many, but in recent years firms have formed subsidiaries for the purpose in order to utilize the Euro-Dollar market. Often, the subsidiary is incorporated outside the United States.

APPENDIX
THE PSYCHOLOGY OF BEING A BANK'S CUSTOMER

Describing the financing of working capital, as this chapter has attempted to do, may provide the reader with several facts or procedural relationships, but unless the *personal* relationship is understood the real-world use of this factual knowledge may be a disappointment.

This is particularly true with an individual's or firm's relationship with a bank. Lest we forget, business is really a "people problem." And

---

[9]The most dramatic recent case of a V-loan arrangement known to the author occurred in 1967 when Douglas Aircraft Company borrowed $80 million through a syndicate of banks, with Security First National Bank (now Security Pacific National Bank) as manager. Apparently the banks were unwilling to make the loan without some sort of guarantee, so a V-loan guarantee was arranged.

bankers, like other businessmen, have problems, particularly with people. In this appendix an attempt is made to discuss what a firm's relationship to his bank should be. But the first order of business is *selection* of a bank; after that is done with careful consideration, the more difficult task of building rapport with the banker must begin.

SELECTION OF A BANK

There are many ways to classify banks, but the following trichotomy is relevant here: *retail* banks, *wholesale* banks, and *combination* wholesale and retail banks. A retail bank is usually small in asset size and is geared to service personal checking accounts. Typically the average account size is $400 to $1,000.[1] Frequently these banks will be located in residential areas (or in the so-called "bedroom communities"). A wholesale bank, on the other hand, is established to service business, export-import or agricultural accounts. Some wholesale banks have an announced policy of not accepting personal accounts, except, perhaps, for the principals of their industrial and commercial accounts; some will accept personal checking accounts as a matter of course, but will not solicit (*e.g.*, advertise for) such personal accounts. A combination bank, which includes practically all the largest banks in the country, has a deliberate policy of actively seeking business and personal accounts. They typically have large offices in the central business districts, and where branch banking is permitted, a network of branches. It is also quite common for these combination banks to be departmentalized into the retail division and the wholesale (with an appropriate euphemistic synonym substituted for "wholesale") division. With large national banks, there is frequently a further division of the wholesale activity into a metropolitan division and a national division. Other banks use industry divisions, but regardless of the actual division a functional split at the main office level is usually effected between the wholesale and the retail functions.

Now the point of recognizing this difference between retail and wholesale activity is critical to the business seeking a good banking

---

[1]There are some announced retail banks that are the antithesis of this. As such, they may accept no personal account for less than, say, $250,000. In return for this exclusiveness, they offer elegant furnishings for their offices, personal attention to every wish, and an appearance that is conspicuously devoid of tellers' cages. (Some states have put a stop to this practice, however.)

relationship. For all too often many small- to medium-sized firms find themselves banking with a basically retail-oriented bank, or with a branch of a combination bank. In so doing they find lending officers who are not fully attuned to their business, and consequently the rapport that is so important (discussed below) is absent or not well developed. Many sophisticated finance men firmly believe that it is better to deal with lending officers who are knowledgeable in *their* business rather than the omnibus lending officer. With knowledge and understanding comes a degree of confidence—a most necessary ingredient if a loan is to be made. Human nature being what it is, it is easier, and certainly safer, to say "no" to a request for a loan, or to an increase in a lending limit.

The choice of the right bank may also be affected by the possible services a bank might render their business customer. Today more than ever banks have a variety of services that run from lockbox arrangements to international banking and commerce facilities. Assistance with mergers and acquisitions is now offered—with and without a fee—by certain banks. Some banks have what they call "money-engineering departments" that have staffs able to assist certain customers with cash management. And the list of services increases every week. But unless a firm is cognizant of what a bank can offer—in addition to knowledge of *his* (the customer's) industry—a firm is likely to use the bank only as a check depository. On the other hand, if a business firm selects a retail bank, or a bank not attuned to his field, these services will be unavailable whether or not the individual firm has a need for them.

ESTABLISHING RAPPORT WITH A BANKER

Once a seemingly suitable bank has been selected—perhaps the firm's current bank—the next task is the selection of a lending officer and the building of rapport with him.

Contrary to popular belief, a business firm does have some choice of lending officer with whom it wishes to work. The hierarchical level of this lending officer must usually be accepted as given, however. If the firm is changing banks (or bankers), going high in the banking organization may produce a choice among several individuals. On this subject, most young businessmen would prefer a banker of approximately the same age, while an older businessman would probably prefer someone not as young. Obviously, this is a matter of individual taste.

After selection of the individual banker is made, the most important job begins: establishing *rapport.* To do this it is necessary, in addition to being civil with this person, to understand a banker's needs and problems. And the singularly most important need of a banker is the need to know what is going on with a customer.

To many ill-informed businessmen, a banker is someone who is to be "kept in the dark." "Tell them nothing" typifies the feeling. Perhaps for some, this feeling has its origin in depression days when a banker repossessed one's family home, or firm, or grocery store. To others, it is an extension of annoyance in completing personal loan application blanks that seek personal and perhaps embarrassing information. Whatever the reason, this approach is diametrically opposite that intended for building rapport with a banker.

Instead, the astute businessman will start by inviting his new-found banker to visit the plant—be it ever so humble.[2] While there, have him meet the staff in the accounting department. At this time, it is appropriate to offer the banker periodic financial statements. Suggest, for example, that he build a file on your firm and instruct your accountant to forward the reports. Usually quarterly data will be quite sufficient. In any case, offering financial statements *before* being asked is the key to the psychology of the situation. If you need a loan, the banker is going to insist on statements—usually certified statements—anyway. By offering them you relieve the banker of the need for requesting them. Furthermore, by establishing your willingness and ability to send reports periodically, without having to be dunned, will assure the banker that while a loan is outstanding you will continue to send him financial statements.

If the firm is engaging in financial forecasting, it is sometimes a good idea to share these forecasts with your banker. Assuming that the firm is reasonably confident of meeting its forecast, it is psychologically advantageous to forecast financial needs, especially if one believes as some that the worst time to ask for a loan is when it is really needed.

SUMMARY

Perhaps the above discussion of the psychology of being a bank's customer can be summarized by the Golden Rule, "Do unto others as you would have them do unto you." To some, this psychology will seem

---

[2]Many able salesmen believe firmly that it is best to get the "weak points"—or sources of possible embarrassment—out on the table as soon as possible. If not conceded early, their importance might grow with time.

all too obvious, but many bankers dealing with customers on a day-to-day basis wish their customers would take this advice.

When a banker makes a loan, he often feels a very real sense of involvement. Furthermore, he has superiors and loan committees and auditors checking on his actions. If corporate (and personal) customers can make his job easier and more efficient, it is only reasonable to expect reciprocity. And this reciprocity can come back in many ways—loan extensions for cause, or loans during periods of strict credit rationing when other less cooperative customers are being denied or cut back, increased bank services, and, possibly, assistance with personal financial problems. If nothing else, a closer, more personal relationship may alleviate a possible point of friction for the harried businessman and banker!

CHAPTER 7

The Analysis and Forecast
of Cash Flows*

INTRODUCTION

More than any event in recent years, the debacle of Douglas Aircraft Company has pointed up the need not only for financial forecasting but for new methods of analysis. To many businessmen the notion that a firm could have too many sales orders seemed anathema. More sales mean more profits; more profits mean greater success. But the road to success must be charted carefully. It is true that in the case of Douglas the immediate problem causing loss of control was a cash shortage, and that the proximate causes were such factors as operating inefficiency, delay of jet engines, and penalty clauses in tight delivery schedules. But the very facts of the case point out the necessity for not only an efficient method of forecasting but a system that would be susceptible of sensitivity analysis and simulation. By this I mean that the model should permit simulation of such conditions as poor operating efficiency or an unusual increase in the volume of accounts receivable, and thereby a precondition appraisal could be made of the financial consequences attendant to prospective management policies or decisions and/or to exogenous events. Furthermore, the forecasting model should be stochastic and thus avoid the basic problems attendant to the straight point estimates commonly used.

The purpose of this chapter is to present a cash-flow format that meets these objectives and provides a framework for *understandable* financial forecasting. After specifying the format and construction of an historical cash-flow statement, this chapter discusses the techniques and

*This chapter was originally presented as a paper before the XIV International Conference, Institute of Management Science, Mexico City, August 1967.

problems attendant to forecasting the cash flows of the firm. Next, a method for sensitizing the estimate through simulation is offered, and finally two simple illustrative models are presented for the purpose of suggesting other uses to which the cash-flow model can be put.

POPULAR TECHNIQUES OF FORECASTING

There are four popular formats currently in use for financial forecasting: the *pro forma* income statement and balance sheet, the "source and application of funds statement," and the cash budget. The projected income statement, if used alone, suffers from an inability to account for changes in asset and liability accounts; and the balance sheet, if used separately, does not reflect sufficient detail of operations. The source and application of funds statement tends to take account of the result of operations, in the income-statement sense of the term, but presents the data in such a way as to project noncash items such as depreciation and retained earnings as though they were cash items. Students and businessmen alike have trouble conceiving of the accountant's notion of "funds" *vis-à-vis* "cash." The cash budget as usually presented by accountants is entirely too detailed, while the source and application of funds statement has been criticized as being too vague.

THE PURPOSE OF THE CASH-FLOW FORMAT

The cash-flow format used in this chapter is the version of Gordon Donaldson and James E. Walter, and many of the ideas contained herein were inspired by their writings or are an extension of their previous work.[1] Essentially, the format is a combination of the income statement and balance sheet, but specifically avoids the inclusion of any noncash charge or reserve account—for example, depreciation, depletion or contingency reserves. As such it is intended for the purpose of analyzing and forecasting the flow of cash and the financial operation of the firm. It is intended neither as a substitute for the income statement, particularly for tax purposes, nor for the balance sheet. Since it is a model of the cash

---

[1]James E. Walter, *The Investment Process as Characterized by Leading Life Insurance Companies.* (Boston: Division of Research, Graduate School of Business Administration, Harvard University, 1962), pp. 367–376, especially p. 368 (Table XI-1), and Gordon Donaldson, *Corporate Debt Capacity* (Boston, Division of Research, Graduate School of Business Administration, Harvard University, 1961), Chapters 7–9, and especially pp. 163–164. Much credit belongs to these authors for reviving this cash-flow format.

inflows and outflows, it has the further advantage of being operational for the financial forecasting of *any* firm, from a one-man shop to the largest corporations, and is effective irrespective of whether the firm is a capitalist firm with a profit orientation or a nonprofit firm.

While such noncash charges to the income statement as depreciation and depletion are most important for reporting income to the tax authorities in the United States and most other countries, and are accepted convention in reporting "net income" to the owners of the firm, it is most important that these accounting conventions not be allowed to confuse or in any way cloud the financial forecast of the firm. As far as the actual cash flows of the firm are concerned, the real effect of these tax-allowable charges is to reduce the income tax, and thus reduce one cash outflow.

CONSTRUCTION OF HISTORICAL CASH-FLOW STATEMENT

The cash-flow format used in this chapter has the following divisions: (1) operating cash inflows, (2) operating cash outflows, (3) the net operating cash flow, (4) the priority cash outflows, (5) the discretionary cash outflows, (6) the financial flows, and finally (7) the net change in cash and marketable securities accounts.

The first three parts—actually one part trichotomized for convenience—deal with the cash flows emanating from the operation of the main business of the firm—the so-called "operations" of the firm.

Part I, operating cash inflows (OCI), consists of sales (S) for the period *t*, plus other income (OI) for *t*, minus a period to period positive change in accounts receivable (AR). Symbolically,

$$\text{OCI}_t = \text{S}_t + \text{OI}_t - \Delta\text{AR}_{t-t_{-1}} \qquad (7\text{-}1)$$

While other income is, admittedly, a nonoperating item it is included here for purposes of convenience only and because it is usually small in size relative to sales.

Operating cash outflows (OCO) consist of the cost of goods sold (CG) for period *t* less any depreciation or depletion that might be contained therein as these are noncash charges, plus selling, general and administrative expense (SG) for period *t*, plus taxes (T) for *t*, and since all of the taxes may not be paid in the period in which they are incurred, a positive change in accrued taxes (AT) from period t_{-1} to t is subtracted. From the balance sheet, a positive change in period ending inventory (I) levels is added, plus a positive change in prepaid expense (PE), minus a positive change in accounts payable (AP), minus a positive change in accrued payroll (APL). Symbolically,

$$OCO_t = CG_t + SG_t + T_t - \Delta AT_{t-t_{-1}} + \Delta I_{t-t_{-1}}$$

$$+ \Delta PE_{t-t_{-1}} - \Delta AP_{t-t_{-1}} - \Delta APL_{t-t_{-1}} \quad (7\text{-}2)$$

Net operating cash flow is defined as operating cash inflows minus operating cash outflows, or

$$NOCF_t = OCI_t - OCO_t \quad (7\text{-}3)$$

Net operating cash flow as defined, is the amount available after the operation of the business, and as such is available first to service the required priority payments the firm must make, and secondly to finance the discretionary expenditures the firm wishes to make.

The priority outflows (PO) consist of such variables, as interest expense (IE), regular retirement of debt such as a sinking fund (SF) and/or lease payments (LP), where the lease payments are of such a magnitude as to warrant separate inclusion other than as an administrative or general expense. Priority outflows are thus

$$PO_t = IE_t + SF_t + LP_t \quad (7\text{-}4)$$

The principal discretionary outflows (DO) are such variables as capital expenditures (CE), research and development expense (RD), and divident payments—preferred (P) and common (C). If substantial advertising expense is undertaken by the firm, this too may be included as a discretionary outflow. In fact, for many firms advertising expense is construed as an investment, and thus inclusion in this section seems quite reasonable. Symbolically, discretionary outflows would be:

$$DO_t = CE_t + RD_t + P_t + D_t \quad (7\text{-}5)$$

The above *sequence* of discretionary outflows is not suggested as being definitive. To some firms, a minimum dividend on common stock and/or the preferred dividend may take precedence over any other discretionary outflow. In such a situation, the ordering might be rearranged to read as follows:

$$DE_t = P_t + D'_t + CE_t + RD_t + D''_t \quad (7\text{-}5a)$$

where D' equals the minimum dividend on common stock and D'' equals a kind of residual or extra dividend that is a function of funds available after outflows for the first four components in the right-hand side of Equation 7-5a. In any case, the *ordering* of items in this expression is not of significant consequence to this presentation. A firm may order the outflows in whatever sequence of priority it chooses. Of credit to this format, however, is the fact that the sequence is readily discernible and top management may choose the sequence they wish—observing the consequence of whatever choice is made.

The sixth section of the format, the financial flows (FF), includes the cash *inflows* accruing from the sale of debt instruments (B) or stock securities (E), or, conversely, would include the *outflow* of cash if a security issue—all or part—were retired. By its nature, this section acts as a balancing device. When large sums are needed, debt or stock issues are sold, or term loans (TL) are effected. If the model is constructed on a quarterly basis, short-term seasonal loans may also be included in this section:

$$FF_t = B_t + E_t + TL_t \qquad (7\text{-}6)$$

The seventh section, the end result of the aforementioned steps, is the net change in the cash and marketable securities accounts (CMC) on the balance sheet. Symbolically,

$$CMC_{t-t_{-1}} = NOCF_t - PO_t + DO_t \pm FF_t \qquad (7\text{-}7)$$

FORECASTING CASH FLOWS

While the construction of a historical cash-flow model for, say, five or ten years is a useful tool of analysis per se, its primary purpose is to provide the data on which to construct a projected cash-flow forecast. And this raises the question of technique. The three apparent techniques available for this are ratio analysis, simple trend extrapolation, and regression analysis. As a working tool, I reject ratio analysis for most variables because of the inherent assumption of linearity and unitary elasticity. It is true that unitary elasticity may be present in the functional relationships, but to assume such a situation in *all* variables is greatly to oversimplify the matter. Simple trend extrapolation is equally naive. The apparently superior method, for most variables, is therefore regression analysis, and this is the technique used in this chapter.

Treating sales estimates as the independent variable—or in this case the parameter—each of the operating variables bears a direct or indirect relationship to sales, except other income. A discussion of the functional relationships follows.[2]

Naturally I have omitted a discussion of sales forecasting as this is a separate subject.

Operating Cash Inflows

From a knowledge of the composition of the other income account, an estimate may be made of this usually minor item. Accounts receivable is regressed with sales and the period-to-period change in each case is observed and entered in the model. From personal observations of several hundred scattergrams of this regression, the fit via a straight line is usually excellent.

Operating Cash Outflows

1. Cost of Goods Sold. Like accounts receivable, the regression for cost of goods sold will usually exhibit excellent correlation, but the forecaster must be aware of a very real tendency for the *ex post* data points to break away and rise upward from a linear-fit forecast in the case of a rapid expansion in sales. This usually results from the common occurrence of bottlenecks and the inefficiency of newly hired workers. If sales were forecast to be lower in the future, it would seem on a *priori* grounds that this tendency to break away from a linear fit would not be evident. Of course, whether this occurs or not would be mostly a function of the speed with which production is adjusted to the reduced sales. If a stable labor force is to be maintained despite the variations in sales of a more or less minor extent, this could tend to flatten out the function. At least some irreversibility would be observed, however, if a stable labor force were expected, because of, say, a guaranteed annual wage contract.

2. Selling and Administrative Expense. If the selling expense portion of this grouped item represents a generally salaried sales force, then this portion will react, probably, quite like administrative expense, and these two items may be logically grouped. If sales expense is strictly a proportionate variable with sales, however, it should be shown as a separate variable. This would be the case, for example, if a straight,

---

[2]For an earlier example of regression analysis as applied to the Cash Flow variables see the Rex Lathe Case written by Jame E. Walter, in Robert F. Vandell and Alan B. Coleman, *Case Problems in Finance,* 4th ed. (Homewood, Ill.: Irwin, 1962).

unchanging commission is paid for each sales unit.

Ruling out this latter case, selling and administrative expense will normally exhibit a regression function that is more flat, *i.e.*, less sloped than the two preceding regression functions. This is, of course, expected because it is rather fixed. If sales are expected to increase steadily and not very fast, simple extrapolation of the linear fit will provide good to excellent results. If, however, there is a sales cycle predicted, or a general sales decline, this function is likely to exhibit considerable irreversibility. Corporate managers may be slow to add to their sales and administrative staff, but they appear to be even slower in reducing their staffs.

3. Income Taxes. While admittedly income taxes are not strictly an operating variable, they are so included for convenience and because the only major nonoperating tax deductible expense is the interest paid on long-term debt and large lease expenses if shown separately in the priority outlay section.

In general, the tax variable must be estimated via a *pro forma* income statement. Most of the items needed for this projection have already been forecast, but the depreciation expense has not. It is with this variable plus the interest expense, that the first significant degree of circularity is evident in the model. In short, the future depreciation expense is a function of past and future capital expenditures. But future capital expenditures are in large part a function of the cash flow available in the period, plus possibly the additional external financing obtained, whether that be debt or equity. Thus a rigorously deterministic solution implies the simultaneous solution of the capital expenditures, debt, depreciation and, possibly the research and development policy of the firm. Since this is not feasible for practical purposes, a heuristic solution to the amount of future depreciation and interest payments must be offered, at least as a first approximation.[3]

In a prior unpublished case study[4] utilizing the cash-flow format, Walter assumed a constant capital expenditures outlay and derived the depreciation expense increment in future years through the use of the ratio of the period-to-period change (t_{-1} to t) in depreciation expense to the difference between the capital expenditures in t_{-1} and the depreciation expense in t_{-1}, and so forth. Thus, if

---

[3]Sensitizing the model through various possible values of the variables in question will tend to relieve some of the doubts caused by this circularity. See the section on sensitizing the model below.

[4]James E. Walter, *Evaluation of Equity Shares: A Case Study.* Wharton School of Finance and Commerce, University of Pennsylvania, no date (c. 1963), mimeograph.

es, it is also possible, with sufficiently sophisticated mulate other events. For example, if management he effect of a variance in any one of the variables on flow, given a point sales estimate, then it is possible rough the use of a control card or by putting in a note terminal. One such card would have a column for iable. If the conditional mean estimate of that variable, y the regression function, is to be used, a 2 could be olumn for the variable. If the upper 3 standard-error limit ould be punched, or a 3 for the lower limit. In this way of several potential situations could be simulated.

APPLICATIONS OF THE FORECAST

imulated the net operating cash flows for the desired future en the original sales estimates and the desired degree of a number of applications, *i.e.*, models, may be developed e projected data. While not attempting to be complete, the models could be constructed utilizing this cash-flow format and cted net operating cash flow.

el I—Forecasting Debt Capacity

some financial theorists, the optimal capital structure of a firm, e debt capacity, is a function of the marginal cost of borrowing *is* the returns from the capital. In probably the foremost article on bject,[7] Eli Schwartz argues that the firm's debt capacity is deter- d by the tangency of (1) a transformation function between rate of n and the market's appraisal of the risk of the capital structure, and market-indifference function between rate of return and the risk of ital.[8] While very interesting from a theoretical point of view, the hwartz model is hardly operational. Even if the functions he describes ld be accurately ascertained (which is doubtful), he makes an incor- t assumption, namely the homogeneity of debt. Essentially there are o types of long-term debt: the kind that is payable periodically with principle due at maturity, and the kind in which interest requires iodic interest plus amortization of the principal through a sinking

[7]Eli Schwartz, "Theory of the Capital Structure of the Firm," *The Journal of Finance*, 14 (March 1959), pp. 18–39.
[8]*Ibid.*, Chart 3-B, *loc. cit.*

$$\alpha = \frac{\Delta DE, t_t - t}{\text{capital expenditures}_{t-1} - \text{depreciation expense}_{t-1}} \qquad (7\text{-}8)$$

and the depreciation expense in period t would be:

$$DE_t = DE_{t-1} + \alpha \cdot DE_{t-1} \qquad (7\text{-}9)$$

In an example employing external analysis, Walter used the mean of this ratio for the preceding years, but were a firm to make a cash-flow forecast from internal data such a perfunctory approach would be ob- viated.

In any case, given the projected depreciation expense, and interest expenses, the pro forma income statement may be completed and an appropriate estimated income tax rate applied to the estimated taxable income. This would provide the income tax expense variable (T_t), and from this the accrued tax variable ($AT_{t\text{ -1}}$) follows from the tax rules. With the change in the tax regulations of 1964, firms no longer have the six-month credit period (for tax liability over $100,000) as they previously had under the Mills Bill of 1954 (See Chapter 6).

4. Change in Inventories. As with other balance-sheet items, the absolute level of inventories must be forecast first, and the change from the prior period calculated. To do this, inventories are regressed with the previously estimated cost of goods sold, if only a simple regression is attempted. Since inventories are also a function of the *speed* with which sales are increased or decreased, a multiple regression using cost of goods sold and the change in cost of goods sold also seems appropriate.

5. Prepaid Expense. Since this variable, which constitutes such items as prepaid insurance and supplies, moves in a rather uneven man- ner, its projection particularly through mechanical means presents some- thing of a problem. Since it is usually a small item, absolutely, the change from one period to the next is likely to be small absolutely also, even if it be large relative to the item *per se*. If projected estimates are not provided by the financial manager, a simple straight-line extrapolation might suffice.

6. Accounts Payable and Accrued Payroll Liability. These ac- counts, like inventory, are most directly correlated with cost of goods sold. Thus the absolute amounts could be estimated by regressing them with cost of goods sold and the period change calculated accordingly.

Having estimated the operating cash outflow variable values for each period, the quantities are summed *algebraically* (remember! minus a negative change means an addition) and the resulting net operating cash outflow, Equation 7-2, is subtracted from Equation 7-1 and the net operating cash flow estimates, Equation 7-3, are thus produced.

CALCULATION OF THE REGRESSION EQUATIONS

Since all of the foregoing variables are highly intercorrelated, attempts to measure the goodness of fit will certainly disclose biased results. But this is true with all such time series work. Fortunately, the results are not impaired because of the admitted high degree of intercorrelation. The processes underlying this model are not strictly stochastic, but neither are projections made of almost any other set of time series.

Before attempting a mathematical fit of the variables it is wise to examine the scattergrams of each simple regression.[5] If an historical datum point seems to differ markedly from a line of best fit excluding the observation in question, then the analyst preparing the forecast should consider why the observed difference occurred. If the reason were something unusual, such as a long strike or an ephemeral war scare, then deletion of the datum point may make for a better forecast.

SENSITIZING THE ESTIMATES

Having completed the above estimates for the desired future period, the model may now be sensitized. While point estimates have been relied upon almost exclusively in the past, they are inherently weaker than range or probabilistic estimates.

Since the estimates of the variables and thus the net operating cash flow point estimates are derived from the sales estimates, the sensitivity analysis must begin with the sales estimates. While many approaches to sensitivity analysis and simulation of this problem seem possible, the following seem to be most obvious and suggestive of other approaches.

The first approach would be a simplified PERT technique. Consider the point estimates of sales for each period that were utilized in the point forecast of the model to be the "most probable" value for that period. Now in addition to this request, the sales forecasters, usually the marketing department of the firm, will supply high and low estimates on either

[5]For a similar caveat on this point, see J. Fred Weston, "Financial Analysis: Planning and Control," *Financial Executive*, July 1965, pp. 40–48, esp. pp. 47–48.

---

side of this "mos
be given such as
should include, in a
values of sales for tha
the "most probable"
subjective probability
be equidistant from the
imply a binomial distribut
ble" value, equal to the mea
(Poisson or Beta) distributio
Irrespective of whether the
period approximately describ
skewed distribution, the mean va
model is computerized, the simula
a goodness-of-fit check could be pro
ple, if it is decided to have only binon
period, a chi-square test could be perf
selected.[6] With the mean and standar
calculated, the model could then be ma
mean and the approximate standard devia
ing cash flow. Naturally, the meaning of
should be understood, for the number of obse
the basic stochastic assumptions usually unde
missing. But if viewed in the proper perspective
could shed some useful insight into the simulat.

The second simulation approach is more per
mer technique. This involves simply programming
for each period, a separate iteration will be performed
principal point estimate plus and minus, say 5 percer
or minus 25 percent might be used as the limit of suc
for each period the simulation would produce 11 estimat
ing cash flow: the original point estimate of sales, five es
and five estimates below. In this case, however, no *explic.*
remarks could be made—no matter how tenuous. The appar
tion would be, however, a binomial distribution of the under.

While the two suggested methods of sensitizing the foreca.

[6]The reader is reminded that a separate test should be made for each peri
entirely possible and plausible for even a short series of sales estimates to contai
binomial and Poisson (or other skewed) distributions.

---

differing sales estima
programming, to si
were interested in t
net operating cash
to simulate this th
statement on a re
each operating va
as determined b
punched in the c
is desired, a 1 w
the joint effect

Having
periods, gi
sensitivity,
utilizing t
following
the proje

Mo

To
i.e., th
vis-à-
the s
mine
retu
(2) a
ca
Sc

fund or repayment of a term loan. In the latter case, the periodic burden may be twice that of the former. I submit therefore that the optimal capital structure—and thus the optimal amount of debt—is a function primarily of the ability of the firm to service the debt. And since long-term important leases require periodic payments, the burden of such leases may be included with the burden of debt in the priority outflows (Equation 7-4) section of the model.

If all of the net operating cash flow (Equation 7-3) were committed to servicing the Priority Outflows, no cash would be available for that period's discretionary outflows, such as capital expenditures, research and development expense, and minimal dividend payments on preferred and common stock. Now this might be an acceptable policy for one or a few periods of time, such as in a severe recession, or because the cash for the discretionary expenditures might be provided from financial inflows. But for most firms, net operating cash flow (here called "3") would be allocated among priority *and* discretionary outflows. If the firm were to make approximate estimates of their minimal (or optimal) discretionary outflows (Min DO) for each period in the forecast, defined in this model "5'", then an estimate of the cash (DC) available to service the priority outlays (here called "3" " would be defined thus:

$$3'' \equiv DC_t = NOCF_t - Min\,DO \qquad (7\text{-}10)$$

or using the numbers:

$$3'' = 3 - 5' \qquad (7\text{-}11)$$

Once again the circularity in the allocation process is evident, but unfortunately, this is a fact of business life.

Since 3" is not a certain sum, but subject to the variance in expected net operating cash flow for each period we could plot the function over time, indicating the 3 standard-error range.

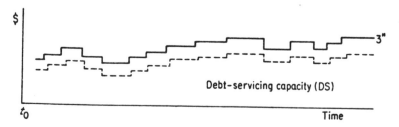

Figure 7-1. The sums 3" plotted over time with 3 standard-error range shown by a dotted line.

As Figure 7-1 shows, the vertical distance from the abscissa to the lower (3 standard error) limit of the plot of the sum $3''$ indicates the firm's debt servicing capacity. Symbolically, if the debt-servicing capacity of the firm for period t is defined as DS_t, then

$$3''a \equiv DS_t = f(DC_t - 3\sigma_{DC_t}) \qquad (7\text{-}12)$$

With this datum for each period, an approximation of the total dollar amount of debt and lease contracts the firm can afford may be made by the following formulas:

If the debt is "interest only" (i) debt, then the maximum amount of debt the firm should undertake, B, is given by

$$B = \frac{DS}{i(1 - T)} \qquad (7\text{-}13)$$

where i = interest expressed as a percentage, and T = applicable tax rate.[9] If the debt has a sinking fund, then this periodic amount $s(t)$ expressed as a percentage of the term of the loan, must be added to i. Thus

$$B = \frac{DS}{i(1 - T) + s(t)} \qquad (7\text{-}14)$$

Through a linear programming model various possible values of B may be elicited by varying i and $s(t)$, within reasonable limits.

Equation 7-14 is also useful in trying to approximate the *term* of the loan if several terms are possible and a target amount of debt is desired. Thus by substitution in Equation 7-14,

$$s(t) = \left(\frac{DS}{B} \right) - i(1 - T) \qquad (7\text{-}15)$$

For example, if 20- and 25-year terms were possible, the s in the former case would be 5 percent, and 4 percent in the latter case.

If the model is to be expanded to include potential long-term lease payments (LP), then these can be added by expressing the yearly lease payment as a percentage of the value L (or as a function of the size) of the leasehold. Expressing the LP as a percentage, called l, then

---

[9]A computerized model would take account of the tax shield occasioned by the interest and reduce 3 (net operating cash flows) accordingly, thus obviating the necessity to multiply by $(1 - T)$.

$$B + L = \frac{DS}{i(1 - T) + s(t) + l(1 - T)} \qquad (7\text{-}16)$$

While these equations are simple, they nevertheless go to the root of the problem and calcuations such as these are natural by-products of the cash-flow format.[10]

Model II—Estimating Required Capital

This second illustration is also a very simple model, but a very practical one. Whenever a new firm is established an estimate should be made of the capital required to finance the firm through the cash deficit period. Apparently, very often this effort takes the form of a *pro forma* income statement, with the initial capital estimated to be the sum of the deficits incurred in the first year or two. But this technique tends to understate the required capital by an amount in the order of one-third. This is so because of the cash required to build up the asset accounts, net of the increase in current liabilities.

If the promoters (or managers in the case of a major expansion of an established firm) have made a projected cash-flow statement of the business as planned, however, it is quite easy to ascertain the capital requirement. In this forecast the financial flows should be eliminated at first. In this case Equation 7-7, the net change in cash and marketable securities, will probably be negative for some time, say three or four years. This is so even through Equation 7-3, net operating cash flow, will be negative for a shorter time; but when Equation 7-3 turns positive, it must still exceed the amount in Equation 7-5 or Equation 7-7 will be negative.

To estimate the capital requirement, an approximate estimate must be made of the cash balance the firm will want to carry. To this amount is added the (discounted) *sum* of the *negative* amounts shown in Equation 7-7. The sum of these two amounts represents a point estimate of the initial capital requirement of the firm. By sensitizing the estimates of

[10]Gordon Donaldson has developed a debt-capacity model quite similar to this, but he uses a different approach to the variance of the cash flow. He argues for the estimation of the effect of the trough of a business recession on sales and suggests that if this trough can be estimated, the overage (*i.e.*, the peak amounts) in good years could be used to cover the underage in bad years. I consider this approach far too risky for most firms because a cash inadequacy with debt service payments means bankruptcy—unless other means of financing the payment are found.

Cf. Gordon Donaldson, "New Framework for Corporate Debt Policy," *Harvard Business Review*, Vol. 40 (March–April 1962), pp. 117–131.

sales and the cash-flow components, a more desirable range estimate may be elicited for the capital requirement.

SUMMARY

In summary, the purpose of this chapter was to elucidate the merits of the Donaldson-Walter cashflow format as a most workable format for financial planning. The overall model presented was a three-stage forecasting model. In the first stage the construction of an historical cash-flow statement was discussed. The second stage is a point forecast of the variables, given the sales estimates. The third stage, an extension of the earlier works cited, is a description of how the forecast estimates might be sensitized according to various assumptions. Also, the deficiencies of point estimates were noted, and a suggestion was made for a modified PERT system for illiciting range estimates of sales over time, and the calculation of the range or expected mean net operating cash flow over the forecast period.

Finally, two simple yet highly operable models were offered as suggested ways in which the results of the cash-flow forecast could be utilized.

SUGGESTED READINGS

Donaldson, Gordon *Corporate Debt Capacity*. (Boston: Division of Research, Graduate School of Business Administration, Harvard University, 1961).

———, "New Framework for Corporate Debt Policy," *Harvard Business Review*, Vol. 40 (March–April 1962).

Schwartz, Eli, "Theory of the Capital Structure of the Firm," *The Journal of Finance*, Vol. 14 (March 1959), pp. 18–39.

Vandell, Robert F., and Alan B. Coleman, *Case Problems in Finance*. 4th ed. (Homewood, Ill.: Irwin, 1962).

Walter, James E., *The Investment Process as Characterized by Leading Life Insurance Companies*. (Boston: Division of Research, Graduate School of Business Administration, Harvard University, 1962).

———, "Evaluation of Equity Shares: A Case Study," Wharton School of Finance and Commerce, University of Pennsylvania, n. d. (c. 1963), mimeo.

Weston, J. Fred, "Financial Analysis: Planning and Control," *Financial Executive*, July 1965, pp. 40–48.

CHAPTER **8**

On the Rationale of the
Lease-Buy Decision

While many articles have been written regarding leasing, particularly since the early 1950's, most have been either descriptive in treatment or simply apologetics on the "advantages" of leasing.[1] It is true that many of these articles served a useful purpose in the five or ten years following World War II, for there was a great deal of ignorance among businessmen concerning the advantages and features of leasing *vis-à-vis* buying an asset. But on the assumption that the reader is rather familiar with the descriptive aspects of leasing, *e.g.*, terms, lease plans, conditions, and sale-leaseback deals, this chapter shall treat (after exploring some misconceptions about leasing) the more interesting subject of whether to lease or to buy a given asset.

To accomplish this, the variables to be considered are set forth explicitly and a generalized decision rule model is developed. Extending previous writings on the subject an approach is made to the quantification of several variables heretofore considered purely subjective or too vague to quantify, *e.g.*, obsolescence and the value of a purchase option at the conclusion of a lease period. Additionally, the problem with point estimates of variables is recognized and a section on sensitivity analysis is devoted to determining estimates of the range of insensitive values a variable might take. Since renting[2] is but a special case of leasing, a

---

[1] A significant exception to this generalization are the two articles by Richard F. Vancil, "Lease or Buy—New Method of Analysis," *Harvard Business Review*, September-October 1961, pp. 122–136, and its sequel, "Lease or Buy—Steps in Negotiation," *Harvard Business Review*, November-December 1961, pp. 138–159.

[2] By definition—legal, as well as commonly used—"renting" shall refer to the situation where an asset is acquired for less than one year. Contracts running one year or more shall be termed "leases." It is true that an asset may be "rented" for several continuous periods together totaling more than one year, but that is merely a matter of oversight or incorrectly predicting usage.

stochastic method of appraising the decision to rent is undertaken as a preliminary to the lease-buy question.

COMMON MISCONCEPTIONS REGARDING LEASING

The Psychology of Ownership

One of the commonest roadblocks to reaching a rational decision to lease or buy is the American tradition that it is good to own what you use. While this psychological propensity may have its place in our personal lives, it is apt to get in the way of profits if carried into the business world.

To come more directly to the point, it matters little whether the firm has a lot of fixed assets on its balance sheet; what does matter however, is the firm's profit (or better, the cash profits). In fact, for any given total net profit the more assets a firm has, *ceteris paribus,* the lower will be its rate of return on investment (ROI). Furthermore, the basic worth of a firm is what it can *earn,* not what it owns.[3]

The Basis of Profit Potential

Consistent with the preceding statement the next question is "What does provide the profit potential of an asset?" Is it ownership? No, it is the *use* and not the ownership of an asset that provides the profit potential that a rational business firm seeks. This is not to say that leasing or ownership *may* have associated with each respective arrangement factors that may provide more or less profit potential, (*i.e.,* say, lower costs) than the alternative means of acquiring the asset. Each method—leasing and buying—does have factors (*i.e.,* variables) associated with it that make each alternative somewhat different. But the essential point is that neither ownership nor leasing, *per se,* can be said to affect the profit potential of the asset in any consistent way.

Tax Deductibility of Lease Payments

An argument often expressed today regarding the alleged advantages of leasing may be summarized thus: Leasing is less expensive because we can write off the whole cost (for tax purposes) in less time than we could if we bought the asset and depreciated it. In the simplest

---

[3]Obviously, there are some unusual exceptions to this general premise, but they should be considered just that, *viz* exceptions.

context, this argument no longer has the merit it once might have had. Before 1954, when accelerated depreciation was approved, it was true that a faster write-off was usually possible. But since then, and also since the IRS's suggested depreciable life schedules have been shortened, this argument has lost much of its moment. Now, with sum-of-the-years-digits or double-declining-balance methods of depreciation, in the order of two-thirds to three-fourths of the depreciable cost may be written off in the first half of the depreciable period. Thus the "tax effect" of leasing tends to be neutralized.[4]

WAYS TO ACQUIRE THE PROFIT POTENTIAL OF AN ASSET

Essentially the only ways a firm can acquire the use of an asset, and thus its profit potential, are the following:[5]

Title Belongs to:	Method
Someone else	Borrow
Someone else	Rent
Someone else	Lease
Our firm	Buy—via conditional sale
Our firm	Buy—purchase outright

While "borrowing" will not be discussed, since obviously it is the least costly, it is not unheard of in business. Many firms doing business with the U.S. government have found that they could "borrow" certain assets for the time of need or the life of the contract. Exotic test equipment, for example, is sometimes "passed-around" on loan from a federal agency or a prime-contractor.

With the elimination of borrowing, the method of acquisition is basically reduced to leasing or buying. But how can a rational choice be made between the two?[6] Since the discussion concerns mutually exclu-

[4]The alleged rationale of this argument is, of course, an allusion to the present value of money. Larger write-offs mean lower taxes, and thus the sooner an asset can be written off, ostensibly the more profitable it is to own.

[5]This list excludes the trivial case where the asset is given to the firm as a gift, and the absurd case when the asset is stolen.

[6]This is presuming, of course, that leasing *and* purchase are possible alternatives. If the asset cannot be leased, that alternative is thus eliminated—but so is the dilemma. Owing to the rather recent judicial and administrative rulings, however, practically all assets can be purchased. Formerly some assets, e.g., certain tabulating equipment or copying machines, could only be acquired via a lease.

sive alternatives for the acquisition of a given asset, no attention need be given to the revenue which will be produced by the asset. Instead, we need only "ascertain" the respective *costs* of each. Even before the variables in the cost decision are determined it is important that consideration be made of the "time value of money."[7]

In order to consider this criterion, the *present value* of a series of cash outflows must be considered. Basically, the choice between leasing and buying may be expressed in the following oversimplified decision rule (expressed as an inequality):

Lease if:

$$\text{Present Value of the Cost of Leasing} < \text{Present Value of the Cost of Buying} \qquad (8\text{-}1)$$

Before proceeding to a discussion of the variables in this decision rule, however, the relation between leasing and renting will be discussed.

THE TIME SHAPE OF USAGE: RENT VERSUS LEASE

In order to determine whether the cost of "leasing" or "renting" should be entered into the left side of the equation, it is necessary to project the time shape of usage of the asset. What is meant by this is best described by reference to Figures 8-1 and 8-2. Here usage, expressed in hours, is plotted as a function of time. Thus, the time parallel to the

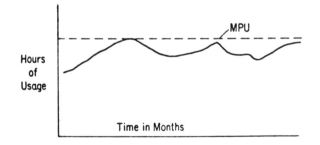

Figure 8-1. Continuous usage.

Conversely, with the advent of lease divisions of manufacturers and specialized leasing companies, practically any asset can be acquired *via* a lease. For example, if a firm's credit rating is high enough, even a custom installed air-conditioning system might be leased.

[7]Since the discussion concerns costs, the present value of a near cost is more than the present value of a distant cost of the same amount assuming, of course, any positive rate of discount. Therefore, the lower the present value of a cost the more profitable that alternative is.

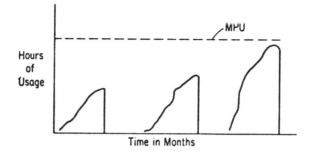

Figure 8-2. Occasional usage.

abscissa, labeled MPU (maximum possible usage), indicates the usable time available to the firm if continuous possession of the asset were the case. The area between the "hour of usage" line and the MPU thus depicts the time the asset is *not* being used. Obviously in Figure 8-2 this area of nonusage is larger than in Figure 8-1 as the asset is only occasionally used. For example, if a firm had need of a cryogenic tanker to supply the fuel for rockets it was going to launch its time shape of usage for the tanker may be as depicted in Figure 8-2. On the other hand, if it needed a tanker to service regularly a research facility its usage would be similar to that depicted in Figure 8-1.

Having an "occasional usage" demand for an asset sets up the possibility that renting, rather than leasing might be wiser—i.e., the alternative with the lower present value of cost over a given period of time. It must be immediately noted, however, that renting is not *necessarily* the less costly, for this decision is a function of not only the expected time of usage, but the rental cost as well. The basis for rental costs, incidentally, is not as easy to ascertain as for lease rates. Generally speaking, rental rates are a function of what the traffic will bear.

If it appears at all possible that renting might be less costly than leasing, a decision rule of the following type should be constructed:
Rent if:

Present Value of the Cost of Renting
$$< \text{Present Value of the Cost of Leasing} \qquad (8\text{-}2)$$

In effecting a solution to this decision rule, it is necessary to determine the expected period of usage per year (since lease contracts are for at least one year, and, usually, are expressed in increments of one year). Moreover, it is necessary to take account of the rental "breaks" as the rental period becomes longer. The following table will illustrate how this can be done.

Assume a cryogenic tanker costing $35,000 and rental rates as follows:

1 month	$3,000
3 months	7,000
6 months	12,000
9 months	16,000
1 year lease	18,000

Using the cryogenic tanker example, a number of firms have purchased or leased enough tankers to take care of their "continuous usage," while renting tankers for the occasional peaks above their (owned-leased) MPU limits. While these rented tankers cost more on a *per month* basis, their tanker usage cost on a *per year* basis may be less.

Determination of Probabilistic Rental Plan Strategies

While Table 8-1 is useful in selecting the "least cost" rental or lease plan where the period of use is known with certainty, the "least cost" plan under uncertainty is only a little more complicated. If it is possible to assign some probabilistic estimates to the various possible periods of usage the problem is helped materially.

Suppose the tanker is needed for a job that may take three or four months or, possibly, even five months. Given this information which plan will, on average, be least costly? Would it be reasonable to say that 30 percent of the time the job will go smoothly and be completed in three months, and a little over half the time, call it 60 percent of the time, the job would take four months, and only about 10 percent of the time the job will run for five months. With this additional information, it is possible to construct a type of "payoff" matrix as shown in Table 8-2.

To select the expected least-cost strategy, given probabilities for each month, the following equation is used:

$$PC_3 = M_1(P_{m_1}) + M_2(P_{m_2}) + \cdots + M_n(P_{m_n}) \qquad (8\text{-}3)$$

where PC_3 = expected cost of a "strategy," *e.g.*, a 3-month contract

M_1 = Least cost for period m_1 with certainty

P_{m_1} = probability of usage for the period m_1

TABLE 8-1   Determination of Least Cost Plan of Rental Contracts and/or Lease for a Stipulated Number of Months. (The "Least Cost" Amount for Each Period Is Shown In Parentheses.)

Continuous Usage–months per year

Rental Rate	1	2	3	4	5	6	7	8	9	10	11	12
Monthly @ $3,000	(3)	(6)	9	12	15	18	21	24	27	30	33	36
3 months @ $7,000	7	7	(7)	(10)	13	14	17	20	21	24	27	28
6 months @ $12,000	12	12	12	12	(12)	(12)	(15)	18	19	22	24	24
9 months @ $16,000	16	16	16	16	16	16	16	(16)	(16)	19	22	23
1-year lease @ $18,000	18	18	18	18	18	18	18	18	18	(18)	(18)	(18)

(Cell figures in thousands of dollars)

Months of Use (with certainty)	*Contract(s) to Select for Least-Cost Strategy*
1	"Monthly" for 1 month
2	"Monthly" for 2 months
3	"3-Month" rental
4	"3-Month" plus 1 "monthly"
5	"6-Month" rental
6	"6-Month" rental
7	"6-Month" plus 1 "monthly"
8	"9-Month" rental
9	"9-Month" rental
10	1-Year Lease
11	1-Year Lease
12	1-Year Lease

In the example cited, the expected costs of $9.4 (thousand), $10.3 and $12.0 for the 3-month, 4-month and 5-month strategies, respectively, were derived from the following application of Equation 8-3 (in thousands).

$$\$7(.30) + \$10(.60) + \$13(.10) = \$9.40$$
$$\$10(.30) + \$10(.60) + \$13(.10) = \$10.30$$
$$\$12(.30) + \$12(.60) + \$12(.10) = \$12.00$$

Here the indicated strategy would be to secure a 3-month rental, with 1-month renewals if required.

TABLE 8-2   Table of Expected Costs of Rental Plans

Expected Usage	3 mos.	Actual Use 4 mos.	5 mos.	Expected Cost
$(p=.30)$ — 3 mos.	$ 7	$10	$13	$ 9.4
$(p=.60)$ — 4 mos.	10	10	13	10.3
$(p=.10)$ — 5 mos.	12	12	12	12.0

Note: Cell values are "least cost" per Table 8-1.

Changing the probabilities for 3, 4, or 5 months to .10, .10, and .80, respectively, yields the following "expected costs" (in thousands):

$$\$7(.10) + \$10(.10) + \$13(.80) = \$12.10$$
$$\$10(.10) + \$10(.10) + \$13(.80) = \$12.40$$
$$\$12(.10) + \$12(.10) + \$12(.80) = \$12.00$$

Thus, with these probabilities of usage, the indicated strategy is to secure a 6 month rental (for $12,000) of the asset.

The expected-cost strategy should be interpreted, incidentally, as the *average* cost of *actual* usage over time, given the probabilities of usage and the least-cost data.

If the user is completely ignorant of the most probable period of usage, equal probabilities may be used for each month. The better the guess regarding the subjective probabilities, however, the more refined will be the indicated "strategy."

Having determined whether to enter lease or rent expense in the left side of the decision rule, attention will now be directed to the delineation of the variables in the basic lease-buy decision rule.

VARIABLES IN THE LEASE-BUY DECISION RULE

It is one thing to state, in a general way, the "present value of the cost...," but it is quite another problem to agree on what does constitute a "cost" of either leasing or buying. Whenever the question of which factors to consider is raised, invariably excessive importance is given to the qualitative aspects. Admittedly it is difficult to deal with strictly *qualitative* considerations in a quantitative model, but it is not impossible. Furthermore, so many of the allegedly qualitative factors *can* and should be reduced to quantitative terms.[8]

Leasing Variables

There are basically only two types of leases: full-service and net leases. If the lease is a full-service lease, then the lessor agrees to maintain completely the property (realty or personalty) and pay all taxes associated with the ownership of such asset. The lease payments (L) will, therefore, represent all cost outflows for the use of the asset. If installation expense (IE) is free to the lessee this item should not be entered as a cost outflow in the lease expression, although it will have to appear in the buy expression. If the cash outflow for IE is the same whether the asset is leased or purchased, IE probably should be omitted and not allowed to make the decision rule any more complicated than necessary.

If the lease is not a full-service lease, *i.e.*, a net lease, then the lessee may be responsible for the maintenance and repair (ME) and/or taxes (TP) on the asset. If these expenses are the *same* as would be included in the "buy" variables, then it is advisable to delete these variables from inclusion. If, for any reason they are different in amount or in the timing of the outlay, then these variables must be included in *both* sides of the equation.

Even though L represents both principal repayment to the owner as well as interest, it is quite unnecessary for the prospective lessee to break down these items. If there is a down payment (DP_L) required under the lease arrangement, this must be included. If the "investment credit" (IC) is applicable, this would be an important variable to consider because the "investment credit" is a bargaining point with most lessors. Since the maximum 7 percent tax credit could amount to substantial sums, the option as to who would take the credit was usually presented in this way: if the lessor took the credit, he would offer a substantially lower (implicit) interest rate, say 3 or 4 percent as opposed to 8–10 percent (1969) if the lessee took the investment credit. If the lessee takes the credit, this expression (IC) need not be entered into both sides of the decision rule for the same reason as was given for IE.

---

[8]For example, the elimination of the trouble and nuisance of owning and maintaining the firm's fleet of trucks is often offered as a qualitative advantage to a full-service lease. But even this can be reduced to a quantitative variable if the answer to this question is delineated. How much are you willing to pay to eliminate the trouble and nuisance of owning the fleet of trucks? Is it worth $1000 a month not to have to be bothered with all the problems? or is it worth more? or less? Thus iterations of this type might in fact quantify a supposedly qualitative factor. (I am indebted to Professor Fred Plotke for his observations on this point.)

Depending on the mobility of the asset, lease periods might be equal to, more, or less than the economic life of the asset. Of more relevance, however, is the amortization period used by the lessor.[9] Usually, once this asset is fully depreciated on the lessor's books he (the lessor) will lease the asset for a substantially reduced rate. In order to take account of these breaks in the lease payment schedule, the first period's lease payments will be designed i_1, and the second period's rate i_2, and so forth. Thus

$$L = \sum_{i=1}^{n} L(i) \ (1 + r_{i_{1\ldots n}})^{-n} \qquad (8\text{-}4)$$

When purchase options are included in a lease contract, a problem arises as to how to take this factor into account. Under the present IRS guidelines, the repurchase price may not be a nominal amount, otherwise the IRS will disallow the transaction as a *bona fide* lease contract for tax purposes. Instead, the lessee may purchase (or repurchase) the asset for a reasonable amount as determined by "arm's-length bargaining."[10]

Of what value, therefore, is this repurchase agreement to the lessee? If the purchase agreement were, in fact, negotiated at the fair market price for such a used asset, then, aside from the expense and trouble of moving out the leased asset and moving in the newly acquired—but used —asset, there would be no value that should be attributed to the purchase provision of the lease. And, of course, the provision would have no value —now or then—if the firm could purchase a comparable asset for less (by at least the amount IE) from someone else.

If, however, it is believed that the lessee could purchase the used asset at a price *below* the expected market price (*i.e.,* without incurring the wrath of the IRS), then this provision would indeed have "value" to the leasing firm. If this is the case, the *difference* (OP) between the option price and the expected market price at year t_n must be included, but discounted back to the present. In addition to this amount, the present value of the saving in installation cost (IE_n) (or moving expense in the case of realty) should be *added* to OP.
Combining,

$$OP'_n = OP_n + IE_n \qquad (8\text{-}5)$$

---

[9]Such a period will be probably the shortest depreciable period approved by the Internal Revenue Service (IRS).

[10]In certain cases the repurchase price may be stipulated if it represents a fair approximation of the expected future market price. Sometimes 10 percent of the original cost is accepted as a reasonable future price at the termination of the depreciable period. Cf. Rev. Rul. 55-540, 1955-2 CB 39. (Commerce Commerce Clearing House Tax Service, Pl. 1382.5522.)

Since OP_n is not known with certainty, a probablistic approach could be taken to the quantity. If the approximately certain range limits could be ascribed to the option value, then increments between the ranges could be established and subjective probabilities assigned to each such value. Multiplying the probability times the value and taking a "weighted mean" of the sum would thus produce the *expected* OP value $(\hat{OP})$.

Symbolically:

$$\hat{OP}_n = \frac{\Sigma OP \cdot P(OP)}{\Sigma P(OP)} \qquad (8\text{-}5a)$$

where P = probability of OP for each discreet increment within the range

Thus OP'_n could be written as

$$OP'_n = \hat{OP}_n + IE_n \qquad (8\text{-}5b)$$

An alternate approach to using mean probabilistic values will be discussed below in a section on sensitivity analysis.

Buy Variables

As mentioned above, the "buy" decision may be dichotomized into (1) an outright purchase of the asset for cash, or (2) a "conditional sale" arrangement where a down payment is made, with the balance plus interest paid over time. It is unnecessary to provide two separate decision rules to take care of these two types of purchases, however. Instead, two variables will be included in the generalized model, and if the purchase is an "outright purchase" for cash at t_0, then the second expression for the present value of the periodic repayment of principal plus interest will simply be zero.

The first variable will be the down payment required (DP_B). If the entire purchase price (P) is paid in cash, then $DP = P$. To be technically correct, the present value of DP, i.e., $\sum_{i=1}^{q} DP_B (1 + r_{i \cdots q})^{-q}$, where $r_{i \cdots q}$ denotes *differing* discount rates in the future, should be considered, but since DP is usually made in one sum initially, the present value of DP is equal to DP at t_0. Thus

$$\sum_{i=1}^{q} DP (1 + r_{i \cdots q})^{-q} = DP_{t_0} \qquad (8\text{-}6)$$

Of course, if there is a time difference between the purchase date and the start of a lease period this fact should be recognized by discounting DP back to t_0 (a point in time common to the leasing *and* buying decision).

The periodic repayments of the portion of the purchase price financed will be designated PR, while the interest payments associated with these repayments will be designated I.

Since depreciation (D) will be allocatable to a purchased asset and amounts to a tax shield, the present value of the tax shield (designated $D \cdot T$, with T the applicable tax rate) must be subtracted from the "buy" portion.[11]

If a straight-line depreciation method is used,[12] and a constant tax factor is projected into the future, the present value of D will be computed as the present value of an "annuity due." If accelerated depreciation methods are used, then the present value will have to be computed as the sum of the present value of each year's depreciation charge times the tax factor. (This latter method will be used in this model.)

If IC (the investment credit) is applicable, then this, too, must be included, unless the lease contract calls for the lessee to take the IC. In the latter case, IC would be excluded from both sides of the decision rule. Since IC results in a reduction of income tax at the end of the year in which the asset is purchased, and assuming purchase at the start of the fiscal year, the effect of IC will be shown as:

$$IC_{t_1} = P \cdot \chi (1 + r_i)^{-1}, \qquad (8\text{-}7)$$

where P = purchase price of asset

χ = applicable percentage that may be deducted from the tax liability of the firm (usually 7 percent).

(Note to reader: At the time of publication, the IC is no longer in effect. The expression is included in the event the IC is reinstated in the tax laws.)

Residual value (RV) of the asset at the end of its economic (useful) life may be of considerable importance to the decision rule. This is particularly true in the case of realty, owing to the widespread appreciation of land and even buildings. If, for example, a firm anticipates that

---

[11]Treatment of the tax factor will be discussed below in a separate section.

[12]Because of the whole notion of the present value of money straight line is a less profitable method than accelerated depreciation and, thus, is *not* recommended.

a certain building will fulfill their "needs" for only ten years, and then a move will be necessary, the RV of that realty will loom large in effecting a decision to lease or buy.

The difficulty of estimating RV has often dismayed decision makers. But difficult or not, an estimate *must* be made. In a subsequent section on "sensitizing" the model, the necessary "closeness" of such estimates will be examined.

Taxes

Since deductible expenses give rise to a tax shield, items of a cash *expense* nature must be multiplied by $(1 - T)$, where T is the applicable income tax rate.

If an asset is sold at the end of its useful life for an amount in excess of the "book", *i.e.*, depreciated, value, then this will give rise to a tax on this profit. But owing to a variety of factors, such as the time period the asset is held, and the nature of the owner's business, the tax may be at the capital gains tax rate, or at the ordinary income tax rate. In this case, an appraisal of which tax is relevant *must* be made and that tax rate (designated T') should be used before discounting RV back to period t_0.

If the firm is subject to state corporate income taxes, then T (and T') should be construed to include both federal and state income taxes.

Obsolescence

In most discussions of leasing vis-à-vis buying, the question of obsolescence is offered as a qualitative rather than quantitative factor for consideration. It is true that this factor is subject to more uncertainty than any other variable in the model, but it is not really the qualitative factor that it is alleged to be.

Instead, obsolescence really means the use of an asset when a superior asset is available. It does *not* mean that the asset is unusable. For example, the advent of the new third-generation computers has made the second-generation computers rather obsolete. But aside from the voguish aspects of having an obsolete computer, the real implication of the term is that there now exists a computer that can do a given job more efficiently, *i.e.*, *less costly.* Obsolescence, in short, refers to the opportunity cost of operating an asset. Many, but not all, assets acquired carry with them the potential cost of obsolescence (referred to as OE).

Admitting the frailities of any estimate of OE, it may be nevertheless necessary to incorporate in the model the present value of such a *potential* expense. Presumably such an estimate would increase the more distant the estimate. But because of the fact that it is necessary to discount these estimates back to the present (t_0), errors will tend to be reduced.

Choice of the Discount Rate

Having identified and defined the variables to be included in the model, the choice of an appropriate discount rate (r) must now be discussed. Essentially the rationale of the discount rate applicable to this model is the same as any other discount rate, viz., the alternative rate of return. If the alternative were to invest in marketable securities, then the assumption of a 5-9 percent rate would seem quite justifiable. Unfortunately the choice is not that clear.

As a preface to the following discussion, however, it is worth while to remember that this model does *not* attempt to assist in the decision of whether or not the asset should be acquired—by whatever method. Thus the question of a minimum rate of return on the investments is obviated.

On the assumption that it is desirable to acquire the asset—somehow, the situation may be simplified to this choice: invest cash in order to acquire the use of this asset *or* invest cash in "another" asset. If the *alternative* rate of return, by investing in another asset, is y percent then this is the rate of return forgone by investing in the fixed asset in question. In short, what is the *marginal* rate of return or opportunity cost?

If the firm is in a position where it needs additional inventory or accounts receivable—which requires the investment of cash—then the marginal rate of return that could be earned by investment in such assets would be the gross profit on a dollar's worth of sales multiplied by the applicable turnover ratio. This might be 30 or 40 percent. If there is not a need for more inventory or accounts receivable then investment in redundant marketable securities (m_f—See Chapter 3) is the best alternative.[13] This return might be only 5 to 9 percent. In general, the stronger

---

[13]"Redundant" marketable securities means those securities which are not needed to service the cash account and are not earmarked for near future needs such as dividend payments or tax payments. In brief, redundancy of marketable securities implies that these securities could be disposed of and the funds invested in other assets of the firm, presumably at a greater marginal profit.

the need for cash, the higher the alternative rate of return—or discount rate—to be used.

Furthermore, since need is, in part, a changing function with time, there is no reason to assume a *constant* discount rate over the period in question. If cash is more in need now, and is expected to be less in need later, then the discount rate should reflect this by being higher in the earlier years than in the later years, or *vice versa*.[14]

This line of reasoning also argues against the use of the firm's so-called "cost of capital."[15] The problem encountered here is a question of marginal cash need and, as such, may be quite independent of the firm's cost of capital.

The problem at hand is to determine the least expensive way to acquire the *use* of the asset. Under the leasing alternative, the implicit interest rate is already determined; under the purchase alternative, it is presumed that the funds will be borrowed and thus the interest rate is included. If purchase is to be effected via a sale of stock then this would be the outright-purchase situation. For those that wish to argue that the new sale of stock would have a continuing "cost," then to the purchase price might be added the present value of this imputed "cost of common stock." The exercise would be quite unnecessary, however, as the present value of the lease side of the equation would almost always be less than the simple purchase price *per se*, unless a very low discount rate is used.

Summarizing, the choice of a series of discount rates for the period t_1 to t_n is a function of the current and anticipated need for cash. While need is, admittedly, a difficult concept to define precisely, it implies the expected marginal profitability of investment in current assets.

If a firm has pressing needs for cash a high rate, say 30-50 percent should be used; if a firm has a cash (or marketable securities) redundancy, a low rate, say, 5-9 percent minimum, should be used. In any case, the rate of discount should change over time as the expected need for cash (or, alternately, opportunity for investment) changes.

---

[14]The reader is reminded that the discount rate used here is quite like the "rate of return" calculated for a proposal in a capital budgeting model. But a calculated *constant* rate would only be constant *ex post* if the *reinvestment* rate in each period were constant and equal to the calculated rate of return. Thus, the use of varying discount rates in this model is, in part, an attempt to avoid the implicit error of assuming the reinvestment rate equal to the calculated rate.

[15]By *cost of capital* I mean the usual "weighted average cost of capital," a discussion of which is included in every basic text in corporation finance.

THE MODEL

The decision rule to lease or buy is stated in the form of an inequality, as follows:

Lease if:

$$L' + [\text{DP}_L(1 - T)(1 + r_{1 \cdots s})^{-s}] \tag{8-8}$$

$$- [(\hat{\text{OP}}_n + \text{IE}_n)(1 - T)(1 + r_n)^{-n}]$$

$$< \sum_{i=1}^{q} \text{DP}_B(1 + r_{i \cdots q})^{-q} + \text{IE}_n(1 - T)$$

$$+ \sum_{j=1}^{k} \text{PR}(1 + r_{j \cdots k})^{-k} + \sum_{j=1}^{k} [I(1 - T)(1 + r_{j \cdots k})^{-k}]$$

$$- \sum_{h=1}^{m} [D \cdot T(1 + r_{h \cdots m})^{-m}]$$

$$+ \sum_{i=1}^{h} [(\text{ME} + \text{TP} + OE)(1 - T)(1 + r_{i \cdots n})^{-n}]$$

$$- [P \cdot \chi(1 + r_i)^{-i}] - [(\text{RV}_n(1 - T)(1 + r_n)^{-n}]$$

where

$$L' = \sum_{i=1}^{n} [L(i)(1 - T)(1 + r_{i \cdots n})^{-n}] \tag{8-4}$$

and

n = intended period of use
q = period over which DP_B will be paid
s = period over which DP_L will be paid
k = period of the loan in a conditional sale arrangement
m = the depreciable period $\leqslant n$

SENSITIVITY AND THE ESTIMATION OF VARIABLES

After injecting numbers into the several variables of the lease-buy model, there is the possibility of taking a closer look at the "guesstimates" used for certain variables, for example OP, RV, and OE. The question at issue is not whether these are entirely accurate estimates of the variable, but rather how much will the estimate have to vary to *change the decision.*

RV, for example, is often cited as a very uncertain estimate. But, if RV is to occur 20 years in the future (t_{20}), and the discount rate is rather large, say 25-40 per cent, the present value *difference* of the high and low estimates may be very little. Suppose RV at t_{20} is guessed to be between $200,000 and $400,000. At $r_{20}=25$ percent, the present value of $200,000 is $2,400 while the present value of $400,000 is only $4,800, or a difference of only $2,400. At $r_{20}=40$ percent, the corresponding present values are $200 (for $200,000) and $400 (for $400,000), a difference of only $200. The point of this example being of course, that it may not change the decision whether the estimate of RV is $200,000 or as much as $400,000. In fact, it is possible, knowing the difference in the present values of each side of the equation *without* a given variable to calculate (since the present value, time and the discount rate are given) the *upper limits* of the estimate without changing the decision from lease to buy, or *vice versa.* Furthermore, combinations of the estimates of the upper limits of several variables may be elicited by the process of iteration within reasonable limits. In this way the difficulty of getting agreement on point estimates of several variables is reduced. Usually, agreement on the range a value can take will be enough to satisfy the inclusion of the variable in the model.[16]

In substance, therefore, the arguments against inclusion of rational variables because "after all, they are only guesses" lose much of their force when the model is subject to some sensitivity analysis. If nothing else, estimates of how *large* a variable has to be to change the decision can be gained.

IMPLICATIONS OF THE MODEL AND SUMMARY

While it is not possible to pinpoint the single most important variable in the lease-buy decision model, it is possible to isolate those variables that probably will play a commanding role.

Usually, it appears, the discount rate r and the size of the down

---

[16]The size of the *insensitive* range in the estimates of the variable naturally increases with either a lower r or a shorter t. If the r is rather low (implying, usually, redundant cash and/or marketable securities) the decision will usually go to buying anyway; if t_n is in the near future, this implies less uncertainty and, thus, consensus of opinion on a narrower range. In either case, therefore, the principle of sensitizing the estimates is vindicated.

payment (DP) will be most critical in the decision regarding personalty. If realty is involved, the residual value (RV) may be quite important.

If r is rather high, it implies that cash is in short supply. On the other hand, if the firm has redundant cash and/or marketable securities, why pay 8-15 percent implicit interest to a lessor for the use of an asset when the firm could finance it at 5-9 percent by selling redundant marketable securities?[17] It would be more profitable to use the redundant cash or near cash items and thus realize a greater yield.

Since the present value of a payment at time t_o is equal to the payment at any discount rate, then as DP_B approaches the purchase price the present value of the whole buy expression rises sharply. But the present value of the buy expression will not equal the purchase price owing to the subtraction of the present value of the future tax reductions occasioned by depreciation charges and the effect of the investment credit (if applicable). The way the model is constructed therefore, the DP_B factor is extremely important to the decision.

It may also be argued that leasing uses some of the debt capacity of a firm and that this is a cost that should be recognized. But to penalize the leasing portion to the extent of such a cost would be discriminatory. The additional borrowing occasioned by the "buy" election would also use debt capacity and, presumably, could also cause higher interest rates on future borrowing. Thus, to recognize this in one instance would require, *perforce*, inclusion on the other side of the decision rule.

To all of the above generalizations, the observation could be made, "yes, but if the other variables are . . ." The point being, of course, that it is extremely difficult to guess at a lease-buy *decision.* The only adequate way to approach the matter is to make actual present value calculations of *all* the relevant variables, and then decide. When rather larger sums of cash are involved, the additional profit gained should more than compensate for the trouble and effort required to make the necessary estimates and compute present values for the variables.

---

[17]This is entirely consistent with common knowledge of business. If cash is critically short a firm would be more inclined to rent or lease than to sink the large sums usually involved in capital asset investments.

Index